Ken Edwards — Collected Poems

Also by Ken Edwards

Futures
Bardo
Down With Beauty
Country Life
a book with no name
Wild Metrics
The Grey Area

Ken Edwards

Collected Poems

1975–2020

Shearsman Books

First published in the United Kingdom in 2021 by
Shearsman Books Ltd
PO Box 4239
Swindon
SN3 9FN

Shearsman Books Ltd Registered Office
30–31 St. James Place, Mangotsfield, Bristol BS16 9JB
(this address not for correspondence)

ISBN 978-1-84861-760-5

ACKNOWLEDGEMENTS

Heartfelt thanks to the following small press operators, some of whom are no longer with us, who were generous or rash enough to publish these writings in book form: Peter Hodgkiss, Galloping Dog Press (*Tilth*, 1980, and *Drumming & Poems*, 1982); Ric Caddel, Pig Press (*Intensive Care*, 1986); Peter Middleton, Torque Press (*Lyrical Ballets*, 1990); James Sherry, Roof Books (*Good Science*, 1992); Paul Green, Spectacular Diseases (*Bird Migration in the 21st Century*, 2006, and *A4 Portrait*, 1984); Ian Robinson, Oasis Books (*3600 Weekends*, 1993); and Tony Frazer, Shearsman Books (for the earlier collections, *No Public Language*, 2006, and *Songbook*, 2009, and also *Chaconne*, 2007, which appeared as a Shearsman e-book); as well as the magazine and anthology editors, too numerous to mention, who gave first showings in various forms.

Cover photo by Elaine Edwards.

Contents

Erik Satie loved children

For June/Des

1975

Postwar

on hitting the
black-&-white tiles
the water-melon
                                burst
pink sugary flesh
spattered everywhere

the clocks stop
"high noon"

dust—

Removals

away into the street the poems blow
west is east & east is west

after all the century belongs to Rimbaud
"you have crushed the grape"

at noon on another street I slough off wrinkles
naked in shark-infested waters

taking a yellow match I set fire to my room
then start again

Coltrane's Narrow Road

the molten rhythm section
              is also   atomized
& that in any case   is the way

your bright new frying-pan
a pale crescent shining

(the frisson I get from Basho)

Four White Pieces

1
matches & fag-ends cram an ashtray
in the stainless steel room
the woman with white logs
poses (wearing headphones?)

2
my eyes big as my boots
my boots & the piano cadence
Erik Satie loved children
look! I'm a lion!

3
a wooden mule & a wooden pig
stand on 9 paperback novels
tomorrow there'll be coffee
& careful words. as usual

4
the toast has melted the butter
the sky has melted the birds
you in the kitchen looking for the cat
me taking the sky upstairs
on a plate

Radio

"see I've mended your radio"
echo of the Big Bang in
Tony's ice-cream bar

The Circulation of the Light

there is wizardry
in what manner & by what processes
stars become dust

Lunacy

scooping earth
for your children flickering
steel flash plane

listening to the
hum of your electric plant-pot
for hours
or behind the gasworks
suddenly being filled with
the lunacy of children

Clickclack

IN from the cold cold night
clickclack
UP the crazy stairs
(feet hurt)

RED
mine's the RED toothbrush
yours is the
BLUE

Three Blue Pieces

1

        one moment follows
another   there's no pushing
chimneys crisscross the channel
        at last   at last

2

            the pale sun
flicks through magazines
tracking their every seduction

3

        sky so very
blue   fizz of 625 lines

if you need me I'll be
telephoning the I Ching

Shell

later you show me one
of them it is whorled
it is hard   it englobed
some pulpy creature
against the bang of the ocean

but now
now it is quite empty

"my sound has no more words"

The Attempt

evenings   olivetti dora

swallows flock into the mirrors
their cries pouring through
sun on your golden skin

coming out as silence

Later Still

later still I looked
out the window   the
street was covered in
glistening fur   how
decadent I remember thinking

Stones

no sound

a handful of stones
tossed in dark water

the ripples expand
intersect then

then

Planetfall at Twilight

curling
silver thread

stars drop
tongues

thigh of the moon
& the crows gather

The Coast Road in September

beating this great drum

over corn-bristles
the foghorn bellows

beating this great drum

Dover

1977

1

spending easter at the farm

grey van parked near
a sparrow incident flashed
by the rutted pools

snow fluttering
smudged trees & grain silos

*

inside   on a bowl by the window
six oranges

2

the duck is
in the oven
stewing in its
own juice

the polythene
clings to the
other side of
the pane

it begins to
snow again
soft petals
of flaked sun

the children
show us the

go-kart they're
constructing in
the shed

a blurred view
of grain silos &
the top of
the lighthouse

"those eggs
are old
the neighbours
used to keep
chickens"

the click
of the door
on brown
dimness

we are not
yet wholly
what we
are

the grass
rippling in
spirals of
grammar

submitting
to this
reality
"this kinship"

warm in the
kitchen
bounded by
the ambiguities

3

the fields are   quite flat
today we saw a moonfaced
barn-owl   broad pinioned
hung in the frozen afternoon
like washing

next   the cows spiky
with straw blinking at us
from their ragged pasture

*

writing this   the sun returns
refracts through the window
onto the TV   blotting the picture

4

picking sea-spinach
hands rooted in clouds
the day has cracked
wild cabbage & rabbits
in the rutted earth
century: 20th: remember that

*

we took a walk to heaven & earth
entering by a rogue wind
not hung on the breath burning
holding hands
tree of skin eating the evening

lesions in fields   the light fading
opening to the cleft of a greybacked
egg burnt purple in the fog
yolk runs down our hands frozen pink
continent: Europe

*

shift of tempo   the grey windows
cold panes viscously preserved
a new order of time
shall pass away
nerve-ends cauterized on the radio
in the throat logic of days
signalling the pulse meal
mossed viscera on the allotment
chalk below day
along the cliffpath

Lorca: an elegiac fragment

1978

"...Even these letters. They *correspond* with something (I don't know what) that you have written (perhaps as unapparently as that lemon corresponds to this piece of seaweed) and, in turn, some future poet will write something which *corresponds* to them. That is how we dead men write to each other."

– Jack Spicer

LORCA / unit one / Starting from Granada

Starting from Granada
we drove athwart the Sierra
treacherous the way
not past Ronda
but moving to the coast by way of
the passes   headed for Motril
            Through steep banked night
past the garages came upon
a sea boiled in starlight
sudden ambience

(12 yrs later the job in hand
to complete this   I read

The history of the Spanish war
of revolution is partly the history
of the abuse of technology

a fiction, a verbalisation
in the moorish city & beyond

                                    the Buick
in which García Lorca travelled to his death
at Víznar… etc   haunts
the metabolism

            Clued into this land

                                    which I call territory
                                    which is a psychic zone & not
                                    geography

I tried for source

writing scouring rock

pressures
terraced in notebooks
salvaged from kelp

In London years later
I'd be in a garden   It is the era
of instant satisfaction
TV & boutiques
                    You salvage
what you can

The territory moved through the centuries
slowly
          the blind territory
                                        spanish
trees yellow oil scum in pools of
fish soup arabesque formations of
sky close textured in alleyways
bread steaming on the dim slabs
sand tufted with grass white as linen
in the disused bullring where dirty faced kids play
garages about gypsy woman follows with
lethargic persistence of thick sky
liquid eyes tiny cobbles with a lick of
sun horseshit   horse flies
beggars doing the street café tables
tucked into rags of skin

the smell of dust   how it was

My lady peels back
the pages & I lie beside her
writing not saying a word
we are here we're alone
in our warm room
in the early
hours surrounded by bones of leopard, lynx
beached in our bodies
by the glacial tide

A room in West London
somewhere in the XX century
the weight of all this, the mutter
of the
radio
the old
man is dying, he has kissed the robe of
the Virgin, but it will do him no good
& I am glad
for all those
who with us tonight
send our
sonar to the
stars

On the beaches
purple with tar the children
point waiting heads

inert the jellyfish lies
beached across the grain
the children drop stones
that slide
soon all this flesh will melt away
rejoin the air

shadows thicken
in the children's mouths
it is late in the century

LORCA / unit two / "the poet assassinated"

In London bread dries in the sun, the morning paper staggers through slots.

I am watching a cat on the garden wall: it pisses an angry dark streak that plummets to the ground, marking a territory, leashed to bricks. Then doorsteps follow me down the street, it's summer, birds twitter in the cathedrals, travelling cranes sink like breadknives into the sky. It could be said that my act is one of definition and exclusion; and that my territory is a triangle: London: southern Spain: New York. The duende becomes the howl of the blues.

The poetic kingdom of Lorca, full of forebodings, threats and omens, is under the rule of a unique and unchallengeable power: Death.

Rock spurts in veins
(they called it history)
a big cream picture crosses the wall
until it is no wall
a thought stumbles into words
& with it the gun& with it
danger

the poet assassinated
the siren in the dream
the endlessness of this road

At Cairo: animals cast in bronze
In Madrid: shooting begins again

under fire from rock crystal
you'd think
Lorca sinks into mythic existence
living still through years of dust
& brilliant deviousness

the air has a sleek pink flavour
as if it were a hollow teat

and yet

Downstreet lamps glare in deep noon
A bicycle tour of the city
reveals
the strategies of madness
signal to noise ratios
expressed as poetry   And who
assassinates the poet?

City turns to absorb cosmic dust
solar flares disturb the outcome
of the experiment, cat on the wall
jumps into hot noon   Wired
vegetables, books, a telephone
litter the table
there are no forecasts left

Bicycle cleaving to flesh
tyres glued to tarmac
the heavy odour of addiction & compromise
Who will name the assassin?

He saw the man in the black suit
He saw the signs

Spoke of a variety of deaths
took refuge in the most unforgettable

A blue rimmed jug brimmed with pictures

Sweet menstrual blood & ceremony
penetrated the flesh
between the shoulder & the left lung

a holy sacrament, a photomontage
of the known & the possible

History, & after that
more history
at an incredibly low subscribers price
no commitment to buy
wars & revolution
cancel your subscription at any time
return the coupon now

Electrodes were implanted
in the thick marrow of the poet
nothing was missed
a pair of shoes   a carpet
the lateness of the hour
breathing
"the persistence of memory"
the tune a violin played
in a hotel restaurant in 1912 in
territory between southern Spain
& northern India, for a poet
shot with opalescence
& the persistence of
peacock silk brocades
on the silver screen
breathing

They implanted electrodes
they who would scorch the page white

Breathing, & after that
more breathing
Munich 1920: Lorca in the Café Lutz
(haunt of Einstein & Planck) let's say
catches sight of the beautiful stranger
in black but he's gone

the marble table tops
are filled with diagrams calculations
(waiters under instruction)

Tangiers 1970:   coffee in a glass
hiding his deformity
under the hood of the djellabah he watches
Burroughs & Gysin
"rub out the word"

everywhere avenues of glory
vegetables or cosmic dust
breathing
Einstein said "We dance to a mysterious tune"
but Heisenberg scotched that one
we dance, he said
towards uncertainty
"it is the theory that decides what we can see"

Uncertainty   Caught in the crossfire
cats howl in the brown night
New York '75:   Guernica
"landscape of the urinating multitudes"
spitting yellow taxis that carry
spoons for the monkeys
Lorca hails one but
the sign says DON'T WALK

LORCA / unit three / "the ultimate cinders"

London 1976:   On this night
of wind of fireworks bleeding in the sky
onto our glass & paper skins

a programme

                    to close the gap
                    to pour
                    unconcerned
from one moment to the next
                    to make the act
of recording equivalent to the pouring
& not separate

                    in other words

an articulation of the whole being
not mere propaganda
or advertising
or entertainment

                    in other words
to admit the duende

The room is hot with bright whisky
mirror slashes the brown air
midnight races across the globe, laps us
tonight the chinese new year

the DRAGON / auspicious it's said
but
2 degrees below zero in my veins
I'm in a dream I'm lost I'm
blue with glory I'm sick
staying in bed all day Saturday
out on the dark roof a newly washed sheet
flutters & flaps on the line against the trees

it's *there*

            & is not   for there is no
year of the dragon
no sheet   & no trees against which to define it
& there is no pouring   & no recording
of that no-pouring

                        just configurations
triggered by the electron flow

call it history

Madrid 1930:
the vegetables of Spain's womb
decay
the hot milk that spurts through her
slowly turns to cheese

1931: a storm of black pigeons
a stairway to grief
no agrarian reform *The countryside*
remained a festering ulcer on the body of
the nation
despite the republic
political contention of light & wind
land still parcelled up
Medinaceli
Peñaranda
Villahermosa
Alba
La Romana
Comillas
the great families
earth occupied by millennial spittle
worked by peasants
for subsistence

death before forty
in the corkwoods

In the fragile days the african generals
Franco   Mola   Valera   Sanjurjo
lurked in the desert   awaiting the call

up this way had come Tariq
& the gypsies
                row by row whose northern cousins
                with caves between their thighs
                half million were to enter
                the incinerators

my grandfather turned the pages
bellowing brass sound
the print smelt of coffee or money, a forward
for Barcelona straddled the goalkeeper
I could not yet read the caption
but it seemed like tragedy

                the gypsies
                an independent migration
                across Europe, a mysterious people
                holders of secret
                signals of nerve endings
                wailers of deep
        song
                bringing knowledge of energy
        lines
                maps locked in
        flesh
                the lost technology of the Sahara

half a million
greasing the machine
with the blessing of our holy mother
etc

1929:
Lorca to New York
spoke often of Blake & Lautréamont

Dali to Paris   later a Falange court favourite
Mussolini, Hitler & british oil money
financing the irrational object
which was to take the place of narration of dreams

the telephone system entirely dependent
on US capital

'34: general strike   miners
in Asturias put down by Franco
with moorish & Foreign Legion troops

'36: the first shots heard across the lines
drifting across the racecourse now laid over

the first victims: Alas, Peset, Formiguera
"intellectuals & dissidents"
engaged in white cheek at floodtide
paradise zone occupied
by clerical fascist savagery

women's heads were shaved & the dance-curve
of water on the beaches found ways to excuse them
their infamous crimes

bishops called it "holy war"   "religious crusade"
while Franco shot Basque priests
in the dance on the ultimate cinders

134 BC: Numantia
defenders set fire to town, wives & children
march out to their deaths, prefigured

then came news of foreign fascist aid
& "non-intervention" of the democratic powers

"at Jarama

in the snows at Teruel

across the
Ebro"

german planes
form an air bridge across the Straits with
Guernica still to come

Sanjurjo, Mola killed
both "in suspicious circumstances"
Franco therefore made Caudillo
Hitler's man

LORCA / unit four / That Banana Moon over the Pan Am Building

1

In the private ecstasy chambers
hot saxophone midnight
three years from the elegant hydrants
12 shrimps in a basket
entertain business associates afterhours

would you believe it

Lorca gets a job as a janitor
he looks the other way
he speak no english but they got
friends in Reno, Nevada
who inhabit jewelled sun rooms
accoutred in all the combinations
they will break your fingers wholesale
no charge

the dude in the black suit they tell him
he's bad   his lips
dangle from his face

Spanish Harlem
the flowers of evil now bloom tattered
between the bricks between
the barmaid's eyes that
telephones would dream of if they could
but telephones cannot dream
they can only sing, she says
as she pours a manhattan
they swallow dimes & they feel no pain
no pain at all

at midnight a sweet melody comes
Lorca brings it hot steaming from the street
he has not been a janitor long
but hopes for understanding before the year is out
at dawn he grooms the slim cadillac
that belongs to the man in the black suit
who wears round his neck
a spoon on a fine chain
next his scarred grey body that he sells
in stylish apartments Central Park West

in the doorway the barmaid
lights another Winston, waits
looks at her diamond watch looks
out into the street
the crazy yellow street
where the stink of the animals
enters the chromatic scale
where the tenor player hocks his tenor
to feed his transcendence
& winds up with all the losers
the sex gypsies in the gas station
where there's never any gas

Summer
no air-conditioning
sun   filthy streets
Lorca striped with light
sleeps
in a forgotten brownstone where somebody years back
hurled an armchair through glass
& it fell seven stories to the street
& they've still not put in the window

bugs & horses
rags of electric satin
a dream of cocaine deserts
"check it out"

2

Some time in the late XX century Lorca returns to New York checks into town quietly   the yellow cab driver the summer-worn cop do not mark his coming
in the papers there is no word
New York you can come out of the closet now, he writes in his hotel room that very night
you're black & beautiful & you're green & lovely & if there are any other colours let them declare themselves now
for just as Flaubert wrote his book with no intention other than conveying that sense of yellow
so the moon rises over Manhattan over glistening Harlem & pronounces it polar
reveals Joni Mitchell dancing with douanier Rousseau somewhere midtown as icebergs approach as
monkeys clamber up & down the Chrysler building, Fritz Lang & gang are there too
make a living trapping them sell them to the tourists
monkeys are your best bet   you can have a lot of fun with monkeys or failing that
you can help assure an adequate supply of energy for all by dragging the swamps every now & then
amazing what you can find
if you come up with 5 or 6 bodies black bodies perchance why that's you set up for the week
& you can cure the angst   & after all
something has got to come right after 200 years of soap operas

Lorca finally gives up, turns on the TV
if he could get rid of those blond clouds that would be fine "I think it's to do with the vertical hold"
or if not there's always history

40 yrs   It doesn't seem that long
a year later avoiding mystics in the street trying not to think about the moon or soap
he remembers the night he lay with the dude in the black suit

who'd discarded the suit so it hung by the sky   whose body glowed white under that moon
in another hotel how they lay not making love lay together touching
& the barmaid in the next room awake her cunt filled with blood
& that too was politics
that they should lie in precisely that way & no other, that they should say what they said, that they should do what they did
that the colours should be as they are
this mystery no saxophone could tell   not even the saxophone of Albert Ayler, found drowned in the East River with nothing left to dream about except endless TV jewels
nor the saxophone of Coltrane who opened another door & caused the people to cry for joy
nor the trumpet of Miles nor the saxophone of Charlie Parker
no this mystery cannot be fathomed so let's just call it politics
when at dawn without a doubt the tenement blocks again take shape become the shape they are
become the shape they have been, restore themselves to space
when in the museum Picasso's masterpiece restores itself to light
& Harlem restores itself to love like a frightened child picked up by its mother
& the sun appears blood sacrifice
so perfect

New York, writes Lorca, you have my undivided attention
instantly feels his rhythm coming back to well
& well all is well or if all is not yet well beneath the savage moon
then at least the possibilities are open right there on the flesh of the sidewalk
but even as he writes there is too much heat & it is not all in the air but some of it burrowed under skin
just deep enough to feel as lethargic persistence
so that the garages the disused buildings have shadows painted with black shoe polish

& still the people of this old city   the hustlers the mystics the intelligent whores
do their washing post their parcels through the long years

dreaming of toilet articles at night dreaming of flesh attachments
dreaming of bodies oiled & glistening on tonight's talk show
dreaming like an artist painting his own blinding seven years in the future
of saliva & peacocks & waiters
& above all the yellow moon that struts its stuff & plays the blues on FM radio & fills Lorca's head with phantasms of science fiction & sees taxis swarm uptown into the fading neon & is so sweet & high & coffee sharp & like some silent ballerina so utterly fantastic

In the early hours Lorca checks out
he takes no luggage
upstairs he has left still asleep the man in the black suit
this time, he thinks, this time
he may just give him the slip

LORCA / unit five / In memoriam (blues)

The war goes on   any war
it happened at six this morning
                        says Hugh holding a teacup
now no. 37's gone

the old admiral blown 60ft
the street obliterated

& where is Lorca now?
                        buried in shale
at Víznar where the forestry department
has planted pines
                        because none would grow
                        & landscaped the area
                        to hide the graves

También se muere el mar

the sea, too, will die   & the levant
blows trails of damp cloud over & up
surfing the rock

Lorca shall we see you
bathed in the earth at Víznar your mouth
filled with blood?
will you come tumbling down
to the estuary where it opens out
to the glare of the oil refinery at Carteia?
are those your shining eyes
across the bay?   & will they be kissed
by the girl drowning in the well?

is it enough to say
that in the density of our dream
the oilslicks reach the beaches
the pines claw at bedrock
& history says
"there will be evil"

but where
are you now Lorca?   maybe in Harlem
not just speaking
from the surface but penetrating
to the innermost core
cante hondo
calling out
from the centre
wailing (is how
jazz has it) of
the vast life
carried within
the bad trips too
the fear
that no reprieve may come, that
we may be locked in the dream
& find no exit

On the morning of Jan 1st
the moon over the rock
revealed a landscape drowned in honey
& the dead bulls of Domecq
dragged by mules to the infirmary
leaving the fragrance of their blood
thick with sex mixed with formaldehyde
& the memory of mountains

on the morning of Jan 1st
we drank our fill &, hungover bleary,
looked on each other & looked
away   because of what we saw reflected
the shadow of white days the
electric meat dream
in the fur of our throats

& we looked in the funny mirrors
in a vain search for comfort
& we looked in the glass labyrinth
& our hearts leapt
all night the floodlit stadium
rang to savage kids' voices
demanding candy

it was 1936

On the morning of August 19th
the love thugs & the armies of the holy ghost
nazi sex kids Falange queer bashers
moved into your skull at twice
the speed of sound
they are moving in still

who assassinates the poet

no records but a death certificate
dated 4 yrs later / "died of war wounds"
mass & holy communion celebrated at Víznar
the certificate no longer issued to the public
and
a Guardia Civil, seeing your picture
after the war, broke down sold your story
but not one of the firing squad had known your name

so much jasmine & nightshade in the garden
that we all wake up with lyrical headaches

In the deep silence of the vegas
the bones lie still layered
the old arab spring still speaks clear
from before the days of the Catholic kings
grass soaks up guttural birds

no words

1975–78
London

LORCA / unit six / Postscripts & prescripts

(the reader may omit this unit if s/he so wishes)

opening quote from Jack Spicer *After Lorca* (1974)

unit one
quotes from Hugh Thomas *The Spanish Civil War* (Eyre & Spottiswoode 1961, 3rd rev. ed. Pelican 1977)

the "old man" is Franco

unit two
The poetic kingdom etc, Pedro Salinas quoted in the introduction to *Poet in New York* (ed. & tr. Ben Belitt, Grove Press 1955)

the Café Lutz in the Hofgarten was a favourite meeting place for the leading scientists of the time

it is unlikely that Lorca was ever there

the Einstein & Heisenberg quotes taken from
An Index of Possibilities: Energy & Power (Clanose Publishers 1974)

unit three
in response to a speech given on 29.1.76 by Carlos Arias Navarro, then Spanish prime minister: "Franco, unchallenged and unchallengeable ... We believe that reform is possible and advisable...." and further bullshit

at this point the reader may like to consult Lorca's essay on *The Duende*, reprinted in the Penguin *Selected Poems*

"Foreign aid from Britain, France and America helped Franco win the Spanish Civil War. The official line of these and many other countries was to make no intervention in the civil war at all. But papers accidentally released from Madrid archives show that key support for Franco was available from the western democracies and giant firms like Shell, Texaco and Rio Tinto. ... Texaco gave credit from the first months of the rebellion on vital supplies; oil companies together provided oil worth £130 million at present prices. Franco also got US jeeps for a cash deposit and £50,000 a month and many things on the London commodity markets: Indian jute for sacks, Egyptian cotton for tyres and Malayan tin for hand grenades."

– *Sunday Times*, 20.3.77

much information in this unit from
Hugh Thomas, *op cit*
Sandoval & Azcárate, *Spain 1936–1939* (tr. N Green, Lawrence & Wishart 1963)

Tariq was the leader of the first Moorish invasion of Spain

unit four
the reference to Flaubert is from Breton's *Nadja*

Picasso's *Guernica* is in the Museum of Modern Art, NYC

the artist who painted himself blinded in one eye seven years before it actually happened was Victor Brauner

unit five
"…I knew they'd murdered me. / They ransacked cafés, cemeteries, churches, / opened barrels & cupboards, / plundered three skeletons for their gold teeth. / They could no longer find me. / They couldn't find me? / No. They couldn't find me." (from *Poeta en Nueva York*)

"the old admiral" was Carrero Blanco, Franco's prime minister, who died in a car explosion attributed to Basque guerrillas

information here from Ian Gibson, *The Death of Lorca* (Paladin 1974)
from which also the quote on the last page

Lorca's grave at Víznar has never been located

Tilth

1980

for Erik, Muthis & Robert

"to the wise man all the world's a soil"
–Ben Jonson

1. Citizen K

I

"rosebud"

or
"I think that if they could live
apart they would be mistaken"

voices
a door slams a foot steps

all the guests have gone home

"the language of privacy, or of silence
assails me"   in saying this
he must mend his life
re-make, find anchorage
in flux, palpably, or shake off
the dead

the original image
that lived, grew thin,
uttered

leaves traces, imprints
on all I can imagine
as if pencilled   or drafted
in charcoal

(in the bath a large spider)

(the light)

II

into the woodsmoke

in a room at evening
by a garden

picture the citizen all the guests
have gone home
leaving coffee & the air
heavy, as if ionised

picture
his room
heavy furniture,
an aluminium frame, a lamp beyond
that's enough:

you might say "verbal descriptions
of an imaginary painting"
were that not inexact as metaphor
for mode or procedure

behind bright white light
of his bright table lamp a green
glow parts the darkness
sword fern points at shelf across reaching
to flowered curtain, points into the light, a green glow
of numerals on digital clock
flickers once, a quantum leap
a window slides shut out
beyond the dark garden slack fence a voice
floats over, the radio the stately
shapely sense of things

and the garden vibrated
with resonance of distant strains

of different blues

& greens   rosebud, he wants
(as if you could) to name *that*
before all this becomes manifest

III

the picture gains
form even as it loses
depth

a railway extends below
& above a cliff   at the top
is belle vue, below
six toy lorries under mackerel sky

allotments begin to race
until the sky is covered by earth
& forgotten
grey fields washed the retina, trees
grasp cumulo-nimbus
an interception
of ocean drifts   & to the south only
stones & pieces
of jurassic gravel remain
as text

IV

cows among grass ignore
claws of scots pine beside the montage

an army has fought here
(he asks for evidence   there is none

a tin bath
left in a field, the skeleton
of scrub, a Mobile Home)

three blue doors later three girls
run, one slightly ahead
only to soon
disappear behind platforms
arrived with new darkness & the crackle
of interference patterns

V

further, glass mediates
blue puddles in mud   frost overlays
grass   Friesian cows
wait at the crossing
it's a landscape
slung between punctuation like the desire
that joins drifts of granite
stopped at points
sunless

VI

not twice five miles, then,
nor accretion
of power
but an acreage of delight
in black earth molasses & clouds
bear down upon the worm

I envy not that man's heart
of a spacious pleasaunce

deposited   private property
appropriated to residence

but this house, & its garden
has moved into its gentle & more beautiful
ruin & undoing
sombre or genial, the precision of a grammar
assigned the safeguarding of the message,
long, slow & complete

& yet never complete, a meaning
opened out   decay space, crepuscular
visions or awakenings
become possible

VII

so the citizen loses
& finds himself
on the edge of a big city
near the silver thread of a railway

and the eruptive blossom on his skin
betokens a culture –

the steam they carried through greenhouses

arithmetic & thrills
in a tropical landscape

VIII

the house
is 4 cream walls, windows chipped black
volcanic glass, slates jammed

in the gutter, & in the loft
bats & those postcards from Venice
those silver blues & greens

there are yards of polished wood
walls sculpted in candlelight & still
I have said almost nothing about it

in the ruined garden you walk
through thicketed traces of scaped terrace
past frogs under scum gloss, hand snags
on a bramble, row of beads

to where a stream discharges itself
at the opposite extremity
& precautions are taken, gratings
of copper or iron at the places
of its entrance & exit

within the curtilage dream property
a short term licence switched around
alignment of his neurology

a broad terrace half as wide may catch
the last red light, blushing with its natural coral
"the purest of all human pleasures"

IX

"I must have some musk & noisette
& jasmine, to run up the mullions, & honeysuckle
& clematis to cluster
as twine among balustrades or fix in the mouldering crevices
& the musk-mimulus springs out of every fissure

"knotted pleach-work & intricate borders
from the orange to the service tree from the stately

hollyhock to the tuft of wild thyme
it repudiates at first glance its vegetable sculpture

"clothed with roots & the earth about them
during a period of 22 years exercised this uncontrolled sway
faced a sea of thistle & bramble
that no gardener trims, dream with what year
these hands will date their letters"

X

a culture, an acreage of delight
the "dignity of timber"

night settled in, he finds himself

all guests gone home, no interruption
to complain of   "I shall see you again"
"I shall hear your voice, we shall take walks together"

it was only the day before yesterday

he works at the window
and there's all that space
and he drank some coffee & whisky and there was recurrence
memories that of a sudden the house generated –
it could be just the smell of polish
on the table at dusk, and there's all that
to come, sword fern young shoots have curled
green pale ends tight put forth blindly

he works, cool green of night
he drank some coffee then the woman
came in with her jokes

XI

apples fill his mouth with sweetness
lunar *sotto voce* strays
through empty rooms where no animals are
snapshots of a cabin cruise fall down
composite video signals fall down
on a polished wood floor   rectangles
of paper are collaged in a way
or showing a procedure
that makes the heart beat faster

just on the vestibule of consciousness
where the sleepy images maintain
walls & towers
when conscious control has been suspended

slowly the bubble lifted

there were machines of various sorts

2. Ancestral Voices

XII

foxes come down from the embankment
I saw one dead in Cuckoo Wood it was pinned
between the eyes grey & ghastly   we skirted
burnt gorse & past Orange Court found
the Farnborough road & thence back
to Lower Green Farm the masts
of TV aerials shining through brushwood

ten miles from the Crystal Palace

interpenetration
of "global cybernetic industry"
the end of movies
the beginning of dreams

XIII

"a dream is the fulfilment of a wish"

first comes the dark wood
where there is no clear view
& it is easy to go astray

then there is a cavernous defile

and then, all at once, the high ground
& the open prospect and the question:
"which way do you want to go"

XIV

winter: clouting the old tongue around

snow on her mouth   headlines make
strange technologies of her generated displays
a little girl is thrown off the train
"no blame"

commuters with News & Standard
before wandering off in ones & twos
waited in front of the glass doors
disconsolately for garbled announcements
echo'd over glazed points

cycle to the station
each morning to inner city Charing X
dirt in a cutting cold steak pie & mixed salad
work & locatory action
accumulated mistakes

fats, edible oils & catering sundries

"a considerable thriving culture of addicts"

Camberwell: overcoats & cider bottles
on the frozen benches

(the confluence becomes wavy
gold floods the garden line, grids
I had forgotten along the way
hair wet & plastered   I make
a shallow drill by pressing
when I awoke there was snow, the texture
inconclusive, home through a haze of sun
& radio chatter)

cycle home from the station

early frosty evening
snow crunch beneath wheels
dark houses curtains drawn
sodium & cats

XV

I act I return I wait for the bus
& all the heavens come down

in south London
there are desperate measures & far from grace
a space a place for marginal growth or death

sarsparilla mint & thistles
among private rituals
an old woman, wandering, desolated
among bright shops   breaks
my gaze, traps me

and with her hands frames me
"you don't need no blessing"
her action is no action
that can be construed
in any but the most elemental
way
"look at this fucking weather!"

an old woman
with soapy hands on a rainy street

with glazed eye
& alcoholic breath
homeless, following the signs
utters…

XVI

THE OLD WOMAN'S MONOLOGUE

"...wanted a belly kid put up
but I won't entertain em
ain't never had a proper life
never lived on the ground floor
I'm waiting for my proper life to begin

"it's Jesus he's downstairs
too late for the situation
that's religion   downstairs smoking
what yer going to do then? same again
I'd be more happy standing on water

"I've no great opinion of mankind

"he can't hear me you know
well he still enjoy a pint or 2 anyway
changing his mind & saying all right let's
try & give them everything they need
well we heard all about this that's how
I classified life before
I had the ECT
but now that it's actually happened
& lord so knock a few off
I been left in the wilderness

"well I'm not *staying* then

"now what has happened in the last 3 weeks
did you get any practice?
what has happened is a collapse
best years of my life
knew what was on then
I've got no happiness in the world
if we now seem about to be changing
& to be   to finally see

our substance in a way
to live my last security   I'm not guilty
no I better watch it
I don't want to

"but if I can afford tomorrow
be all over in 3 weeks   or 3 months

"& be evicted by the council
no shoes
feet are wet
2 girls   it's a bugger   no I wouldn't
my only regret is I spent so much energy
worrying about what could happen
ah sit on a hot stove & then will not
try to change kids' eyes as much as possible
stupid not to have lived every minute
I'm such

"it's going to help break up
up on your bloody moors
I went up this morning she said she's moved
back into an hotel
well animals do it
I've got to the pitch now I couldn't care less

"this place will be treated
exactly the same as any other
or won't be long collapsed
I took some keys I was trying doors
I forgot about 2 centuries

"if I've said it before I'll say it again
how old is she? starving maybe
she's 19   I don't know what to say
bloody dog
if you don't come with me they said
you've made yourself homeless
do you like me?

"this may mean a short time in a hostel they say
you get your dinner
& they've told you

"go on
I'm hardest rock"

XVII

old woman in realms unknown
of approximate notations

of the apparent world of time & space
hospitals, deserts, cliffs, theatres –

endless waves of flaking matter
peel away from the silhouette

comfortless &
with no lines that the mind could grasp –

looked into my eye, sometimes
just past

clasped then
my hand
once more uttered
& was gone

and then a family group approaches
down the street, he tall & strong
she blonde, smiling, the pram…

closer   & veins flower
in his face, he carries
an empty cider bottle, staggers

her hair is brassy, she's teeth missing
their laughter is forced, the pram
is filled with waste paper

XVII

idiolect & ritual, spilled gravel
undaunted blessing, I wait
for a bus to Caledonian Road
I cannot stand this life I can
not I buy seeds
I buy compost & netting

February:
geese swimming in the canal

XIX

in Camberwell a man told me
of another dead fox
in a garden he'd reclaimed
where he was aware of a texture
tilled fine, become text,
strata, sifted

consciousness beyond our imagining

at this hour   even then

rake over the bed
to remove surface
& then at right angles endless waves

the lower part of the house is dark
I check to see is there any back to the door

hold the handle, peel away
sift fine & pad down the seed bed
fat glistening earth at a steep angle

late winter Sunday: vixen
crosses the garden
& disappears beyond the gate, leaving traces
in the snow
traces

XX

behind the dark forest
the express raced in a stream of yellow
intermittent light
to the coast to its secret orbit

XXI

rain
the world in fragments
pieces of sky scattered over
the allotment

between the branches
bone shines
the skeletons of birds & mice their waxy skulls
their blood & fur in the furrows

a cat watches
from afar its stone eyes gleam
I follow
a little way into thick brambles where
it retreats   cheated

rain falls slow explosions
fill the garden stalks harden
at the tips push out blood red buds
and summer is a child's kite
in the field beyond
the dark
three trees
mulch packed up against
rain falls

thistle is winning the race

a world in fragments

XXII

MID-LATITUDE SOILS

podsol
grey & brown forest soils
prairie & degraded chernozem
chernozem
brown & chestnut soil
brown forest soil

break it up a little

XXIII

rake over the bed
to remove surface stones

then rake first
in one direction & then at right angles
till the soil is quite fine

in this raking
hold the handle of the rake at a low angle

if the rake is held
at a steep angle to the ground
the surface is liable
to become wavy instead of level

with the garden line
mark where each row
of seeds is to be sown

along the line
make a shallow drill
by pressing the rake
handle into the soil

or use the head
of the rake to make
this depression

XXIV

on the train
I observe daily the progress
of gardens

rows of lettuce (*lactuca*)
in ground infested with bramble & thistle

a non historical approach
a reliance on
"what we are & continue to become"

the lettuce is one of 48 genera
of the order *compositae*
to which also belong the thistle & dandelion

(we is presumption
that unexamined nostalgia
for public experience
the cultic, the total
the complete, the
too inclusive)

the lettuce is the
“legitimate” usurper
of that space
rank weeds are the rest, the gardener decrees
as voices outside a culture

XXV

allotments

cat white black
arched over fence

a wrecked hearse in a
back garden

XXVI

voices wash up cold carriage glass
the language of privacy, southern railway
generations of dust ingrained

all of a sudden a train jerked I fell over
I fell into the gap

the voices

XXVII

UTTERANCES

"inna living room I've got insulation
pink panels if you didn't know
but we know it's there
different rolls & that
them gotter decent flavour
put it over the top
but we know it's there see

"lung cancer
they will not do nothing

XXVIII

"my mate went on the machine
now with about five fifty
I come out with one twenty
was that in the railway club
I was working with him Sunday
went into a pub Maidstone West
Saturday night went down the Bell in Ashford
I would've thought bugger
make it yourself
my mate played snooker   was a shop steward & all
by the time he gets back the lights gone out

"them chaps they go bump bump
breathe down the line & they start moaning

XXIX

"they've got all these dank great rooms underneath
downstairs   under neon
veins actually recorded
furniture
semi detached this sort of place
at that price is very cheap
makes you wish you got 2
we've already got the utmost stink
surviving the moon

XXX

"I got one of these sun rovers 2 year ago
the whole thing built
on funny farm
any stains
you give spin & enjoy it
otherwise you save it
we're not really concerned with leaving the kids
but we were seriously thinking
of getting one of these nudity stuff
the odd time we got up to town
you could smell the energy
a treat"

XXXI

June
brings
the end
a garden
of delight

opens it out

returns the history
of "human nature"
to another place that is
uniquely here
a garden "not enclosed"
an inclusiveness a version
of the real,
ecstatic, relinquishing controls
that seek accumulation of joy
& exclusion of all that is other

XXXII

cabbage run to seed
leaf cold yellow grey
summer morning
beetles chew the white rotted meat
the rain held off

XXXIII

spiral tendrils of marrow
search, suck air
don't find anchorage in thick
deep red podsol

marrow's self seeded, barren a year
came up unseen in the box
in the white sun

horizontal dance curve I seek out
in sun such perfect line

XXIV

in hot dry weather spinach bolts
flowers, reverts to type

XXXV

each day spent weeding, tending
beneath the concrete post where
there is no longer a bird hut

dandelion   bramble   the glow
of photosynthesis among the grasses
I root out their milky spines

they grow from the roots

fluted panels of neon bright red

warp, wobble & dance

arrangements of rose
stems, the halves of one circle split
burnt sienna

a vortex display
cerulean blue, Mars red, rose madder & black

the roots go deep
a sense of tension & vertigo
is established

XXXVI

UNTIDY CONDITIONS OF SITE AT LOWER GREEN FARM

Dear Sirs,

I have received complaints regarding the untidy condition of the gardens at the above premises.

An inspection has been made and it is considered that the complaints are justified. The trees, bushes, and other vegetation within the curtilage of the premises have been found to be grossly overgrown and the boundary fencing is in need of repair.

I would be pleased therefore if you would take steps to improve the condition of the site by 2nd October 1978, failing which I will have no alternative but to consider instituting formal action in the matter.

Yours faithfully

Borough Planning Officer
London Borough of Bromley

3. Singing of Mount Abora

XXXVII

…Then the woman
came in

he slept by a garden
under river, dreamed, skin pale as milk
of a journey through Africa
in separate carriages
that ended in a shitheap   imagining's compost

they spoke Spanish there, in the
"dark continent" of unknowable
terror pleasure out of time
out of synch, deep

a vision in a dream

"arranged in such a manner
that the grand khan, sitting
on his elevated throne,
can overlook the whole"

they breathe through the night
she & he, intertwined, the house
a sumptuous movable feast
founded in the fine tilth
of circumstance

XXXVIII

time returns, light

fade up on the cypresses, the hinterland
seen last year in snapshots, many years back

the light
generated by past time, filtrate
of images that allow no choice
"all pasts shall be coeval" brilliant
unearthly dreams 24 times a second
"the truth" a set of frames
as determinants of an elusive present

XXXIX

people in a house
lives in a book

random moments of peace

your life was all before you
because the real news flooded back
& allowed you this (certain snapshots
were not like the world)

this unpredicted action
self seeded in the sun   will pass

she walked to where you could look over

sound of the sea

XL

the single viewpoint
tyranny of perspective
the formal garden

decays, or shall we say
dissolves

gasholder, valves & tubes

an encircling
ocean of thistle
flowers purple
waves in storm of summer

and the moon
as pale fragment in the sky
of a hot summer morning

XLI

ceaseless & blest, the fields
turn past the railway, towards opacity
keep flowing
with a tenderness measured in isobars
digress
into a texture, almost

sexual attractants of butterflies
are secreted by the glands of abandoned locomotives
with their fires still alight

but you're always brought back
to British Rail's belly bared
to the big scarred ceiling
of cloud that spreads up
from the Kentish coastline, suspense
now packed & twitching in the
muscle & meat of "everyday life"
laundry, gravel for fishtanks, plastic sacks
are components of that grid
sulphur, meat & maximum penalty

PURE-PAK, push to open, unsweetened
pure jaffa orange juice, coffee in a plastic cup
with small beaker of creamer
larkspur on the rushing banks
through unclean window gorse bush the skeleton
of a tree, they throw their rubbish here
the conversations the mood music family shopping
the matched sights: feathery bright

XLII

a butterfly trapped in a glass jar
hitting & flicking its wings, acts out
at first separately & then jointly
the whole scenario

XLIII

when he returned unseen a year later
to the house, entering
its specificity of dreams
without end or alternative as it seemed
the time was not long until its final decay:
a shudder of straw, bats, dry rot in the loft
mice, bird droppings, darkness

when he is guest, the most
ordinary objects are sombre
in their cloak of presence that soaks
up the bright light of their pulse

the squirrel, the fox
are absent in dense growth that defies boundaries
blurs marking, tangles
together the days of summer, those dendrites
& axons firing memory as Rimbaud

is An Other   the cat
remembers him, though, comes
to be nuzzled
through the burnished foliage daintily

there is a city
between them, there are 2 bars of music
a page of soft earth   "I feel it"
the world's all disordered & lovely again

XLIV

snow had
melted into
the ground
stiffened it
with premonition

the idioms employed
are those of marketing
suppose the whole stanza
the whole poem
were an extension of
control by naming?

XLV

in a house with soaked spongy rafters
the citizen makes certain slow transitions
in a series of artificial frames
from violence to elegance by way of indeterminacy
spins music off a random page, off the
"live & technical fibres of grammar
impacted language, glottal verse
bursting out of eden

the heroine falls in love
with a phantom from her past

& he is left with this impression, no
not even that
no lasting comfort
only measureless delight

XLVI

afternoons mostly a wash
of silver grey & maybe
through a window
apples   almost ripe

XLVII

towards the light, towards
thickness & immensity
vivid with the relish of reading
thunder scarred through chaos & night
to shatter Cosmos
dissolve thinking into haze
perturb thought, put the mind in touch
propose penetration
of fact transmuted   in state of flux

to demolish predication
of extremes   to invite in
the forbidden   slicing bread
uncorking bottles   talking in ordinary tones
over the edge of the possible
with large wine glasses to hand
to show more clearly love
& conflict

XLVIII

towards the light, through stem
& leaf, through photosynthesis
through dialectic through the body
when thought is allowed to sink
creating in some thaumaturgic fashion
out of nothing its world
for the time would fail me to tell
of unexhausted opulence & play
were I to venture to shape

XLIX

towards the light, to danger,
where every
idea is a partial idea
to note disparate metals
extraneous meanings
in a cup of milky tea, in a detail
from a ghostly canvas
where amber, time & space
carefully lovely
begin to decay towards the light
where the work streams out
untrammelled lets loose
all one may delight in

L

towards the light, six seedlings
in the space between the panes
south facing forth push
green shapely bursting heads

clear as if etched on a pearl, interweave
"like a nest of startled snakes"
above & to the right
of where he sleeps & dreams & severally is
that which I might almost call
myself, the citizen

LI

is this redemptive, he asks
forks food into his mouth
to wake from the nightmare
to music & touch
new white stones?   already
it's passing

the stones represent perhaps
the ones you love

I don't know

the spider still sits in the bath

and then out on the permanent way
of a morning
charred sooty track, fresh
with a touch of woodsmoke

out of the tunnel & into the light

LII

he is the polished
bird that hops into your mirror

a steel hairgrip in an otherwise
empty drawer

he eats his breakfast
from a pale blue bowl

in the mirror white
woodsmoke covers the spaces
between trees

he has disappeared
into the smoke

LIII

milk white light
floods a window in winter

as if heard from far

turn the earth over

"stop the world"

Begun in September 1977, near Orpington, Kent, and
"finished" in November 1979, in south east London.

Drumming & poems

1982

John Coltrane, Live in Seattle, Impulse AS-9202-2

"You must change your life"

Utterance: any continuous stretch
of speech or writing from a single source

Attendance: to what is there
& what is not there; activational.

Resistance at all points: to corroding
of ideology by "the natural"; to procedure

that carries prescription, that
doesn't enact or become

bed, flower, decomposed into
the stain of collective extasy.

Linton Kwesi Johnson, *Forces of Victory*, Island ILPS 9556

The Firmament Doth Shake

Or the light, or the
Figure itself. Monday morning, not

Reggae boom, the big lorries
Thunder; as sleep glues eyes.

In your own words to
Make music, building Jerusalem in

England's (Inglan's) green & gorgeous
Wastes, the car lots filled

With floodlight & all the
Smoke you can see. Skin

Stretches, & cars are driven
Thro' grilles, matt lustrous &

Matt, Colour Separation Overlay, you
Bet they'd judged them seductive.

Wake to flutter & sun
Full-blown thro' the rainbow

Arch, wake bath'd in the
Irradiated TV meta-language you

Already speak, sclerotic with direct
Juxtaposition of unrelated events, kiss

Kiss No Problem you just
Climb into the heat &

Nothing's happening, nothing at all.
You have choices to make,

Decisions to take, but fluid
Boils in the lungs, the

Vocal's out of synch, they
Whose only concern is your

Health have committed millions to
Screening, attack, erode all the

Way down to the one
Poor fucker, Waterloo surgical spirit

Drinker, savouring his fumes &
Root of anger; under the wine

Coloured railway arches, the shapes
Emerging. The desert is all

Around & the towers shake
When they promise you anything.

Burning Spear, *Social Living*, One Stop STOP 1001

"Elevator"

The street's below, unofficial, unauthorised,
drawing energy & information from a universe

of linear events. Richness is dead
or merely hibernating, there are moves

to improve & enrich the lives of those
who passed through it. I went to visit a couple

who were artisans & working their way
logically to the top. Let's call these separations

reasons to look after & patronise, few
thought them beautiful in a world

I was perpetually leaving & going back to.
That Sunday, mathematics

carried me through, starting further
outside my head than ever before

in a kitchen with dishes of rice,
vegetables, sauces, brought into slate

shadows lengthening & overlooking the back –
the front half kinetic, a course

logically determined & converging
on the syllables of its own

intertwining fibres. The separations
outstrip reality, but the street

remains, a deliberate ending or turning away,
an energy of needing & making.

Eric Dolphy, *Out to Lunch*, Blue Note BLP 84163

Waterloo Bridge, towards Westminster

Big hollow's a most curious sight: the point
at which, loaded & pulled out,

he retreats, liable to topple,
play trumpet, misunderstand

everything. Water circulated
by a show of organdie, standing

& echo'd 'neath bridge soot,
slamm'd doors, recognisable & too soulful

velocity – pipe down – (he looks sharp,
trochaic trammels, well dressed,

tuxedo pale & delicious nodding).

*

Silver sliver standing he looked back

taking in all this
over river, "yes, crippled"

but "very intelligent", "articulate", "witty",
city, gnosis, district, words.

*

At the heart of the work's sound world
all, any or none of the directions

may be followed. 'Cross honey stave
ritual accompaniment, long looping

figures across water, under steel
jabbed; thalidomide, taxi, fluted

& spaced columns, the County Hall,
eggs, wherries, hospital, copper.

Field of force flowed through
to & past the seat of Govt., mixing it

in parking bays & echo blue
appropriate device. No sound now

but Commerce by capillary action
by trumpet blurting & basted

under wintry sky, the heat
of anyone can imagine.

Archie Shepp, *On This Night*, HMV CSD 3561

near the Elephant & Castle

Rain quickens, "sheets
by exhalation, no.3 reed

and settled against the elements
of sound", layered

vibrated by a column that is
thunder & warm cloud;

rough white walls warmed
the body, a house, secured

Otis Redding, *Otis Blue*, Atlantic 588036

Old Man, Camberwell

1

I went straight from school
in England I know nobody

bother me I think
naturally, but I do

stutter, just from temperament.
When most people were

people if anybody
like the freedom of

vast walks, sometimes over
the moment for the past it

drives me up the wall.
On the gas fire, proper

hot food; I'm pretty
introspective by nature, so I have

a radio I don't need
for about 5 years and I

cook at weekends when I cook.
It's a ridiculous

bedsit I'm living in
a room with a bloke

I haven't been
from my childhood.

2

I don’t have any
cold shoulder, but I’m

reading nobody ever
in my furnished

digs; we have a drink
so of course I

didn’t go about
you see if you don’t.

Trouble is my
drink actually makes me

turn to, so I just
see one should have a fund

not a picture, not even
just on the spur.

From any inhibition
men blanch.

John Coltrane, *Selflessness*, featuring
'My Favourite Things', Impulse SIPL 522

Poster, Walworth Rd, winter '80

(A down & out addresses the Daily Mail lady)

In the autumn you
bathe in oatmeal. Your strong but attractive requests
arrested the decline
into sleep & the other half
of print fruits.

Look at the
valuable kitchen accessories;
now they suddenly united,
snorting. The colours
are branded goods,
products which recognise & respond to
human needs.

2 pints of lager
was laughing in your sleep,
flutes of your bones
picking the ball out of the back of the net.

Been away a short while,
out of circulation,
wanting a language an ocarina
a human universe.
But I see you

Flutes of your bones
resonate & bruise,
flutes of your bones
fade away into mere shadows.

*

Confess; the projected ending,
flighted in ways
& changes of direction
that even non-semantic elements or eventualities hadn't thought of,
charges you something horrid.
Gulping drinks
below the tall brick walls
you refrained from cultivating
the now proverbial umbrella;
it's not unusual
nor even erotic.

The message is if you want it
you've got it.
Scrape some clouds & see. St Moritz
or whatever. Clouds of milk.

Flushed face, nocturnal sweating,
101 ways with railway sleepers,
soft furnishings, prints, light & onyx
draped over your shoulders.

What remains of what once appeared essential
draped over your shoulders:
a minimal intent.

Sleep, in your
silk in your silhouette
of sheer deferred gratification.

The things you love
are not rational.

The things you hope for
are impossible.

The mind that you cherish
will degenerate

Sunny Murray Trio, *Live at Moers-Festival*, Moors Music 01054

Geraniums, south London

1

Geraniums   lip blossom
rustles, whereon

the city sky almost white
space.   Children

smelling subways
lead & rain speckled glass.

One healthy plant the rest ruined
at ground level & far away the

sun   behind fronds; two swallows
driven through sunshine, music teased

its appearance slowly till there's
        cardboard   clamped beneath

walls of galvanised iron,
moulder'd bricks

cupped over the lot
or perhaps 2 figures moving but

in coloured sweaters, a woman with
trousers held by coloured wool

down draining crocks onto the flutes
roots tinder   mashed into bone

into a cylinder of yellow grain
volcanic heat, ochre, sulphur.

Geraniums, distorted. Not with
blush lustre soiled   Geraniums

seen through lattice
of heavy iron. Butter melts into

riot as rain
& soil; hardy cactus unknown

to flow it does anyway.
What kind of sickness, a hard man

rehearses his *fin de siècle* over dust shadows

at midnight, so rearranged.
"LBC, it's 17 minutes past 9"

and then nothing but fourteen
people (one for instance

species rubber   flesh frayed pink
"it was not without interest")

2

It gets colder as you leave, children
& only to be expected.

start of winter
a composed text changes

"loveliness" an epidermal itch,
Little

pantiles which undulate, grass run
by the way, geraniums

out of shape by interference
but *through*. Only one

                                   plane prepares   to land
                                                                so many

bills posted crooked, piles of
patterns; a walk

                                                                The click
            drunks beat dustbin lids, the piss

fruit worm eaten, a concern with
coloured felt tip pens crowded

                                             ; fine calligraphy;
catch the bottled light splashed

                                                                bubbles crawl
                                                                thin paper

shutter'd cinema, to get it
you can go *too* far.

nothing to be added, a 5 year stint.
Geraniums, my children dancing

Gato Barbieri & Dollar Brand, *Confluence*, Arista-Freedom AL 1003

Up To and Including (Charing X ➲ Elephant & Castle)

Up to & including the travelling
crane moving slow across white grey

evening sky clear air it's a
human web, ineluctably

tensile. At the bus stop
the red faced man wearing suit no

tie Golden Virginia hanging in hand
holds forth happy babble chatter.

On the bus top dock the ageing
irish teddy boy with half bottle of

Bell's sticking in hip pocket harangues
"respectable" black man on friendship

& the ruling class while black man II
gets on, in hat, has huge

sharp cassette radio held, turns the
volume UP and DOWN, green 123 red 1,

yea KULCHUR, in the maddening hub
flung from corner to corner. And the irish

man makes his way back down the
aisle & off, whereupon up goes

black man II to sit w/ I, saying
"who's ya friend?" All the while

the spanish girl watched, a still
centre, & has said not 1 word.

Paul Butterfield, *Paul Butterfield Blues Band*, Elektra EM 7294

Portobello Road

Fruit, fakes, clothes & classical terrace
in search of 60s style,

Rasta men with communal gardens,
ladies poking carded veg;

by green steel roar sitar players, the
outrageous grandeur of fortunes

inside-out, & just beyond the flyover
looking like Father Xmas with

iron spiral rings, a parrot, wild
& sloping with stucco. You can also explore

almond colours but the mansions are badly damaged
by their own sophisticated charm.

Roscoe Mitchell, *Solo Saxophone Concerts*, Sackville 2006

"What the razor knew"

1

An event is gone as if seeming to become. The cusp, and the depth of structure. "Musical rain-forests", council property, value of which how does it come into being? The cat laps milk and remains and sits, lights out; prismatic moment as if without mishap. On the floor of any structure, music, metre, matches sound debris, pattern'd communality; in a hum an event is gone and passes and is gone and passes. Verbal pleats slip through, beads beading no and yes.

2

An event is gone – "musical rain-forests", council – and sits, lights out. The cat sips milk on the floor of any structure; the cusp, and the depth slip through beads, communality, in a hum. Property, value of which, of structure, how does it come? Music, metre, matches sound debris, pattern'd into being as if seeming to become, and passes verbal pleats. An event is gone as if without mishap, beading no and yes, and remains and passes and is gone.

3

An event is gone on the floor of any structure. How does it come, property, value of which sound debris, pattern'd and sits, lights out, and remains and passes? Verbal pleats. The cusp, and the depth. The cat laps milk, slipthrough beads; into being music, metre, matches, as if seeming to become communality. In a hum, "musical rain-forests", council beading no and yes, an event is gone – prismatic moment – and passes, and is gone. Of structure; as if without mishap.

4

An event is gone at the beginning; how does it come into the story, sound debris, pattern'd long crystal cliffs? It is true and remains, it makes no call. The cusp, and the depth of the past slip through, beads in disconnected flashes, music, metre, matches with the last image: communality; in a hum, that attention was enabled to slip, beading no and yes. The associated images followed one prismatic moment to the memory of structure. To this day I can remember.

5

An event is gone; sound. Debris, pattern'd, slip through, beads the cusp and the depth with the last image. How does it come, of structure beading? No, and yes: long crystal cliffs; it is true. Into the story, and remains communality, in a hum, in disconnected flashes that attention was enabled to slip; it makes no call at the beginning to the memory. The associated images followed one music, metre. Matches to this day. I can remember, of the past, prismatic moment.

6

An event is gone with the last image, and remains long crystal cliffs. It is true that attention was enabled to slip, slip through beads of the past to the memory. How does it come, the cusp, and the depth of structure? it makes no call, communality, in a hum at the beginning, beading no and yes. Sound debris, pattern'd to this day, I can remember the associated images followed one (in disconnected flashes) prismatic moment into the story: music, metre, matches.

7

An event is gone through the sound of the drum and remains, like how close, that attention was enabled to slip, to take care of the past like the heartbeat; how does it come, the capacity to change the rhythm of structure? There is a particular rhythm that identifies itself to communality, in a hum, a variety of accents beading no and yes. People began talking. To this day I can remember, did he play anything superfluous in disconnected flashes? His conditioning places him into the story; his playing suggests freedom.

8

An event is gone. That attention was enabled to slip. Of structure; how does it come? A variety of accents and remains, into the story. To this day I can remember to take care, like how close. Of the past; beading no and yes. There is a particular rhythm that identifies itself to people; began talking like the heartbeat through the sound of the drum his conditioning places him. Did he play anything? Superfluous communality. In a hum, his playing suggests freedom, the capacity to change the rhythm in disconnected flashes.

9

An event is gone, a variety of accents of the past to take care. People began talking of structure, the capacity to change the rhythm. His conditioning places him and remains; how does it come into the story? Like the heartbeat, beading no and yes through the sound of the drum. To this day I can remember that attention was enabled to slip his playing. Suggests freedom, did he play anything superfluous. There is a particular rhythm that identifies itself to – in disconnected flashes, like how close – communality. In a hum.

10

An event is gone, carrying on the investigation of the past from the ambiguity of our judgements. People began talking, to analyse the structure and capacity to change the rhythm structure. Every artefact is a product, and remains through their performances into the story produced by their activity, beading no and yes. It is thus a structure. To this day I can remember almost nothing; his playing suggests freedom, implying a virtually total "freedom". There is a particular rhythm that identifies itself to be sure of impeding this development, like how close crystals would have to be classified.

11

An event is gone – people began talking into the story – and remains. It is thus a structure of the past. Like how close? His playing suggests freedom to analyse the structure and, from the ambiguity of our judgements, the capacity to change the rhythm. To this day I can remember, produced by their activity, almost nothing; structure. Every artefact is a product carrying on the investigation; be sure of impeding this development, implying a virtually total "freedom". Beading no and yes, crystals would have to be classified through their performances. There is a particular rhythm that identifies itself to...

12

An event is gone; it is thus a structure. The capacity to change the rhythm, to analyse the structure and almost nothing into the story through their performances; be sure of impeding this development of the past and remains. Like how close? Structure: every artefact is a product to this day. I can remember carrying on the investigation. His playing suggests freedom. People began talking: crystals would have to be classified, implying a virtually total "freedom" produced by their activity. There is a particular rhythm that identifies itself to, from the ambiguity of our judgements, beading. No; and yes.

Bob Marley & the Wailers, *Natty Dread*, Island ILPS 9281

Short-life property, Bayswater, mid-70s

Cried softly,   with the tin horse
early outside a darkened room

A cat rubbed
against glass

the night the clocks go back.

I have the postcard
in the sooty yard.
Implication
drifts, respected by no margin.

Basement, empty. & burnt. Writing

A quiet week ended in a bang.
We suddenly departed, coming back
& living.
The enigma kept its
subtle ironic ways

we occupied the houses, availability
rubbing shoulders with need.

THE PROGNOSIS

"A good time for reflection,
"detecting likely sources,
"matching the time required.

"Write & contact, be thick skinned,
"clarify. Trust takes a long time,
"do not present yourself as a failure."

I could see lights going on
                                        in all the houses.
                    Sean, I said, I
have no words. He stood, a residue of tar
beneath stars on waste ground estate
beside Henekey's broken window.

He's taken back, & says
Believe what I'm going through.
(was covered by boards, decayed paperbacks)
                    It's hell, he said
through cold pipes, squat &
honey coloured. It would not
console me if the Hierarchy
had it come to then after 2 years,
fuckin' volumes & mould, I need
a place I can dry out, & shit in equal measure.

But I was thinking
                    & if I could have my things
                    & be able to live as if owning nothing

First day, had signed on
for there was no work.

                    2nd day, had taken an axe
                    flung it. What
                    was he doing this for?

                              And when first arrived at
                              Paddington saw a line of taxis
                              Sure I blessed meself, he said
                              I thought it was a funeral.

And he told me about his gold hair & the
scandal it had raised in the arabian

continent.   The girls he'd had!
Repeated the line about the funeral,
you could hardly miss talking with someone
in the room.
And he confided in me
                            "The gold was in the sisters
as if it were clay locked in the basement,
boiled my long fingernails.
                            But the sisters can take
this terrible curse away."

And sometimes   Kenny are you a man?
                                         ah y're not a real man.

                                         I'll fuckin
                                         throw you over.

But I paid no heed to his stories,
I let these things find themselves in a
blaze deemed to be made up of people
I cared for, mellow thudding
metal bath for reflection,
2 green fishes moving
on the lung.

                                         But he took what I cared for
                                         & turned it into my anger

& left me nothing but my anger

                                         oh natty natty,
                                         Natty 21,000 miles away from home

                            Sean: I don't want to
see you again. The transparency's
too bright; he spoke the weird Jah music
went on for ever. I could see lights & a
terrible curse. And my anger was
intrinsic knowledge;

the transparency's intrinsic knowledge.

And one time he's locked the woman
in the basement, with smell of gas, his piss
weeping 'mid burnt pans, gas seeping
through pipes, indian fringed filth
pattern'd rug bursting alight,
                                                                        the many
armed black idol!
Not the clipped arpeggios nor
Dolphy's clarinet against Hutcherson's
vibes so moved me
as when that woman spoke,
her eyes in heat
                                        swayed & bucked.

She told me of the mallets & said
about his gold hair, & they can rake
away all this, she said, I don't
want this.

My anger was a desert speaking.

And her eyes said, You'd take that chance
too, though how would be in the air.
Her eyes like 2 fish.

                                        Trust takes a long time.

                                                        Shrivelled tips of spider
                                                        plant leaves arched in heat
                                                        gas fire hot varnish
                                                        on the chair leg ink in glass
                                                        smudged on card
                                                        concomitant to the ink I
                                                        do believe in.

                                                                        2 cats
                                                        stretch & tense &

place themselves in the room
demand a cheese sandwich.

But that was the source of my anger.

It didn't stand. Yellow
painted kitchen, half empty
dented my palms, from the window
to the tradition.

I cared for him as though
he were my brother.
When he sent the postcard
the rooftops froze.

But I saw him a year later,
not moving, a fat one
down Portobello, in leather
hat, talking.

No feeling

Hawk in the sky

Laughter

The right time
is never the right tine. "Something
comes into my ear
& I write it down."

They've tinned the houses &
prized the metal
that can be traced back above the roofs,
the delicate flash peninsular
residuum of stars & fire
black memory.

The Hierarchy, I mean

But I have the postcard

& it burns.

Albert Ayler Trio, Spiritual Unity, ESP-Disk/Fontana SFJL 933

Southall

Many people shouted to them, to stop and looked very strange.
I was in my garden & I saw this quite clearly this boy was standing

and was left unconscious he sit down protest in the garden when 2 police
rushed past him one of them hit him dropped down I got a glass

hit me on the head with entire area round the Front meeting.
I tried to run & told him like this: Move! and he managed to get

to his feet & it dropped out of his hand couldn't speak then he just
tried to sit him down; as they chased these other police came running

to break up the line of people & started to attack hoping to organise
in response, cordoned off by thousands of blocks & rows from

the western end of the Broadway from 2 blue police at the junction
in a very bad state and one of the police came over

attacked & hit in the testicles sitting against the wall in the early
morning streets in the centre of Southall.

Steve Reich, *Drumming/Six Pianos/Music for Mallet Instruments, Voices & Organ*, Deutsche-Grammophon DG 2740 106

Drumming (Slow Return)

1

Stranger in a strange land,
men controlling entry,
hold the pitiful shoes.

Terrorise the subways,
it's us or them they say,
ecology of the street
TV's frozen music.
They murdered a black race
by commerce & crossfire,
a racist mob, monsters,
a double disclosure
that paraded the flag.

Their heads, shaved to the scalp,
were divided in 3;
who dare talk of "freedom"
in my lungs.
And the british people
straight, with the fingers shut,
who could shout with his voice,
taunted spastic black child
just to stop from being bored.

Who inspected vaginas,
british movement skinheads,
even those who had yet
by commerce & crossfire
to look outside or to
anything "we" elect.

They murdered a white man
and the fists in the air
and he was a teacher
underneath "our" culture;
the swastika hidden,
easily interrupted.
Of racial chaos and
TV's frozen music,
liberation crushed riots
with the dust of pollen
to bloom on a dry day,
fuzzed writing on concrete
police station, all that
shaved into his hair.

Home, school, shop or office.

23rd April
1979.
Men controlling entry
in my lungs. Guaranteed
to be arrested. Young lads,
british movement skinheads,
of the asylum's clientele,
mentioned schemes & orders
which had been submitted
and the heart will follow
anything.

To bloom on a dry day
in the english springtime
to re-direct the flow.

Life we could be living.
Fuzzed writing on concrete,
the swastika hidden,
aerosol'd swastika.

Who inspected vaginas,
who dare talk of freedom.

And the trial was rigged
and everyone condemned
with the dust of pollen.

And the trial was rigged,
a sign of things to come,
and everyone condemned
even those who had yet
to be arrested.

And the british people,
nature of the gestures
and the hands in the air
straight, with the fingers shut . . .
"I'll speak of geography",
anything. "We" elect
a racist Mob, monsters
who dare talk of "freedom".

January '81.
And the british people
were divided in 3,
the swastika hidden
underneath "our" culture,
TV's frozen music.

Hold the pitiful shoes.

And the trial was rigged,
is a trajectory
in the english springtime
life we could be living.
"Zombies will roam the streets",
terrorise the subways,

it's us or them they say,
a sign of things to come.

And everyone condemned
to re-direct the flow.

2

They break up the motion.

They buy the metal and
sell it. The machine
didn't have any guard, it
should have a guard. Many
people shouted, I saw
this quite clearly. They buy
the metal that didn't cut.
You have a machine like
a plane, put it on the
moving belt. You have to
fill out a form, I have
to take up the metal
and feed the knife, wash it
and boil it for pigs, left
handed crabs. Making a
market the rest cut.
It shock me and I decide
not to buy it, them are
more worthier over there
than over here. I cut
the celery, cutting
up metal, I have to
take up the metal with
a knife, just pulled my hands
straight into the knife.

When I came to this country
I see them sell sweet weight

metal to the machine,
scrap metal yard, it have
a piece of wire inside.

I still prefer to have
my fingers than the house,
but the wire didn't, and
chops the metal so the
weight of what didn't cut
comes down and up, and
chops the metal.

Metal and feed, I have
to take up the metal,
you got two wings and the
body, it comes down and up.

The one at the bottom
don't move down and up.

There are two blades just pulled
my hand, I working on
a machine to help load
a lorry with engines.
I feed in the metal.
One reel is shown twice and
dropped in an area of
my mouth. It stand still, the
foreman come, the machine
didn't have any guard,
just the top one move,
I scream out metal yard.

They break up the motion.

3

They break up the motion
just to stop from being bored.

When I came to this country
and boil it for pigs,

they break up the motion
by commerce & crossfire.

They break up the motion
straight into the knife.

Liberation crushed riots
straight, with the fingers shut.

And everyone condemned
who could shout with his voice.

They break up the motion
to take up the metal.

And he was a teacher,
straight into the knife.

Liberation crushed riots
with the dust of pollen,

taunted spastic black child
to take up the metal.

And he was a teacher
with the dust of pollen.

They break up the motion
straight into the knife.

They break up the motion
with the dust of pollen.

And everyone condemned
to take up the metal.

They break up the motion
and boil it for pigs,

who inspected vaginas
to bloom on a dry day.

And he was a teacher,
straight into the knife.

They break up the motion
by commerce & crossfire.

And he was a teacher
to bloom on a dry day.

I feed in the metal
to bloom on a dry day.

Who inspected vaginas
in my lungs.

When I came to this country
with the dust of pollen,

when I came to this country
who could shout with his voice?

They break up the motion
straight, with the fingers shut.

When I came to this country
to take up the metal

I feed in the metal
straight into the knife.

When I came to this country
straight into the knife,

they break up the motion
and boil it for pigs,

taunted spastic black child,
didn't have any guard.

They break up the motion,
didn't have any guard.

And he was a teacher,
straight into the knife.

When I came to this country,
didn't have any guard,

taunted spastic black child
straight into the knife.

Taunted spastic black child
straight into the knife.

And he was a teacher,
straight, with the fingers shut.

They break up the motion
and boil it up pigs.

When I came to this country
straight, with the fingers shut,

I feed in the metal
with the dust of pollen.

I feed in the metal
and boil it for pigs.

I feed in the metal
to bloom on a dry day.

Liberation crushed riots
straight into the knife.

And everyone condemned,
didn't have any guard,

the one at the bottom
who could shout with his voice,

who inspected vaginas
straight into the knife.

They break up the motion
with the dust of pollen.

They murdered a black race
straight, with the fingers shut.

And he was a teacher
with the dust of pollen.

And he was a teacher
and boil it for pigs.

I feed in the metal
to take up the metal.

They murdered a black race
with the dust of pollen.

And everyone condemned
straight into the knife.

They break up the motion
with the dust of pollen.

They break up the motion
to bloom on a dry day.

Liberation crushed riots
in my lungs.

I feed in the metal
by commerce & crossfire.

Who inspected vaginas
straight into the knife.

And he was a teacher,
didn't have any guard.

They murdered a black race
to take up the metal.

Who inspected vaginas
straight into the knife.

And he was a teacher,
straight into the knife.

The one at the bottom
by commerce & crossfire,

and he was a teacher straight,
with the fingers shut.

They murdered a black race,
straight into the knife.

When I came to this country
didn't have any guard.

They murdered a white man
to bloom on a dry day.

4

“The blow had split his skull
from its base to his right ear.
People holding the new
citizenships would be
eligible to have
passports describing them,
splintering the bone &
bruising the brain to
a depth of an inch.
It will be necessary
to restrict the right of
entry to each of them.”

Evan Parker, Derek Bailey, Han Bennink,
Topography of the Lungs, Incus, INCUS 1

East Anglia/Dover/London: "personal politics"

Collage on the telly, installed
for the duration. Expensive moonlight

& was looking for a place to stay.
We'd found a dead one, desiccated,

caught, spurted – smoking the last,
swooping over shifting shadows

of the allotment. Busy printing, state of mind
rapidly become piecemeal, correspondences

between structures before she went
to see her parents. I didn't even know

any handicapped people! Itchy with soot
not vegetables, faces gold, neutron

& electron, a pain in the arse,
starting to start.

*

There were pine-cones & apples
in a bowl, stones on a

mantelpiece, high patchwork,
icons, a poem. Were we being

impossibly naive? Ebullient yet derelict,
we were coming to a crisis, & me

rather embarrassed by it all.
It ocurred to me that it would happen again.

She sat on the damp leather
cushion; read a book; asked me

to help her persuade her. There was
a peach-tree in the garden, soon summer would start.

*

"As usual" operation, the job during the week,
not a prospect I relished. Little

did we foresee. Time on our side.
Partly to deal with, partly to avoid.

Electricity building up, looks like everybody
happy, onset of dusk; wanting to start.

Intensive Care

Poems from The Radio Years 1982–85

1986

Fore Words / In Time of Impending War

Everybody's running to the dark side

over the corner
round the bridge

across the immense
mysterious cities. What if

the world should melt & burn
from the horizon

By order

Disappear

But our love is real.

Following the researches of Hertz, Guglielmo Marconi discovered in 1895 on his father's estate near Bologna that electromagnetic waves could be made to travel between two metal spheres, one connected to the ground and the other to a metal can on the top of a pole. A year later, having made an apparatus that could be used for sending wireless telegraphic messages, he introduced his invention to Sir William Preece, chief engineer of the British Telegraphic Service. By 1897, he had succeeded in sending radio signals a distance of four miles; in 1899, he sent them across the English Channel, and in 1901 across the Atlantic.

"With the passing decades radio waves were generated by human beings with ever increasing intensity. Those that could penetrate the upper layers of Earth's atmosphere did so, and as a result there is a sphere of radio-wave radiation swelling out from Earth in every direction." (Isaac Asimov, *Extraterrestrial Civilizations*, 1980). Thus, we live near the centre of a radio/TV sphere that is expanding in radius by one light second every second. Putative inhabitants of a planetary system round the star Zeta Tucanae, for instance, could even now be watching the first run of "The Phil Silvers Show".

South East London, early spring. The sky darkens: bands of purple cloud against indigo. A 747, on its way in to Heathrow, catches a golden glint on its wing from the now hidden sun. Navigational lights wink red and green; communication between the pilot and the tower vibrates through your body. You get up from the brightly lit desk and cross the darkened room; immediately the television picture (South African police discharging gas canisters) distorts and ghosts. Your heart beats faster as you put garbage into the system. Something hits the nine o'clock news with plenty of blood and plenty of colour. You move in the room, interrupt the signal; you're an interference source. A light goes on in a distant window. Scotland Yard have issued this Photofit picture. An undefined variable has been used. The characteristic interference patterns determine that no centre can hold. Your heart beats faster, and suddenly you realise this is because you inhabit an electromagnetic field, like a vast library under the sea. The telephone rings; you pick up the receiver, but there is no message, only an unbearable electronic screech. Sudden heating of thousands of tons of air...

El Hombre Invisible

I am working in almost complete darkness
just below where aeroplanes ply
back & forth beyond the buildings into brilliance
that could be described as
"unearthly".

And the gaps between the buildings are in strange positions
but I accept this without question
as I accept the radio waves
that penetrate are enveloped by
this room

which is connected to other rooms where the lighting
& all other electrical circuits are arranged
for comfort – call it enclosure –
predicated on certain rhythms – call them
repetition.

But I do not switch on the light & somehow
beyond a given point this becomes a statement;
I am talking about a specific situation
or would be were I not perhaps just
playing for time

totally oblivious but not really
to facts whose presence I could not
possibly have determined by recourse
to direct induction – & already I am nearly there
united

with radio waves with precipitation
of lead & other heavy elements
as one with commercial flights that ply all night
above my head across the sky into the brilliance that will shortly be
all that remains.

Their Daily Island Life

So then they began to explain. And we may say that they have been explaining ever since … And as I say we are still in the shadow of it.
– *Gertrude Stein,* What is English Literature

Behind the wire
stand one or two
or maybe twenty saplings.
And these & those are in bud
& will green
but the three at the corner
refuse

No public language
That is fit

There was a country
buckled by heat & rain, corroded
emerald
near the shore

a long time. I have tried (he wrote)
to knit fragments to make
coherence
of sun that beat once on a wall
and the arrival
of the radio repairman with
pipes, loose wire, yellow oil
brilliance, the bark

I began to name them then.

•

No public language that is
fit for such a time. No further
than a street where plywood
buckled by heat & rain, corroded
gaping dormer set in

bricks cooked soot &
worn by wind, will words go.

The walls are not rose, nor peach
but stained, sulphurous I mean
the brick.

Makes a fire, makes a fire
in the hospital grounds old man
takes a walk on the path.
The pond is no pond at all
there are no benches
but the boys like to ride their bikes
up & down
            up & down
                        up & down.

Behind the wire

•

I have known people
whose language is public & pursues
or attains coherence.
Their house is too hot & is full
of beautiful things
Beautiful
And sometimes
But never mind.

There was a country
(the walls are not rose, nor peach)
behind the wire past the one
who lives alone with her
child & the one who lives
with the quiet one.
Oil in the puddles, makes a rainbow.
Trail of, trail of.
Step in a cardboard saucer,

coherence...
And the corpse of a pigeon
left by the kerbside emerald
at its neck. There was a country
where the language was fit.

It was always behind the wire.

Yellow oil of a dog,
the walls are not rose, nor peach.

And the sun goes down, far gleam &
makes a fire
through my window at the end
of a day of incipient summer
dust veiling the nuclear
brilliance, the bark
of a dog, shouts, ebbing
slow & loses itself among the walls &
buildings, the garden.

These will bud & green
Those will refuse.

I have known these people.
Some who live alone
some with their forearms
encased in leather, some
from the hospital or from
over the sea.
But there is a thing about them
I can't tell.
The rain begins to come down
soft, on a summer's evening
in the city, where car lights move.

Intensive Care

(starting from a line of Shinkichi Takahashi)

This woman must survive
But how can I tell her
That she must stay with what she has
It's an assembled world a shoe here
A shoe there
To stay with such chaos
And be an artist
Or grow more afraid
Walk down to the cold rose light at the corner
And buy a bottle
Awaiting release
Of the afterimage
One year from today this woman
One day from today

She is concerned for her child.
There is another, playing in the yard.
Wave her on her voyage.

The voyage of the child her secret history
Told to no-one but a few imaginary rabbits
And snails traversing the mould
Infected carpets in a deserted building
Spring showers interference patterns have haunted.

Delicate bones of the child; bones
That shield the critical marrow.

You remember them, those days
Inclusive of different
Paradigms, lights off, gestures, mysterious
Shapes at night in the room & nothing to cohere
To wake in a sweat again in the room
To call out
in the early dark in a sweat no light line

Under the door
Spring night cat cries in the distant garden
And stillness after, or just the clock maybe.

It's the imagination that's been sick from rumours
Of a bullet posted through a letterbox
One stormy night the
Red tail lights incendiary
Glow they're going to talk about
Everything you'd better watch.
Big Bang theory goes out of the window
All returns to the one
Frenzied accumulation a
Golden dream discharges
Monetary horses along the avenues that lead
Inexorable
Crowds from the empty hospitals the towers
That crumble slowly into a river
Of menstrual displacement of all that is not
One.

Through a door, via broken window
Spring came early this year
With a bronchial choke like starlings in the engine
Blocked combustion but
Surviving
This body this touching, invisible, in the
Margin that's there.
Which is
Where the child plays
Dressed up in musty stuff from a forgotten basement
Taffeta silk rag wool
Stuff that makes visible.

As the beautiful petrochemical trap the industrial
Diagonals lurch, precipitate
Lead fall-out with the dew
So the voyage
Ends, & begins.

Stars butter skin pores dead leaves pressed
Into the carpet in the abandoned house
Stone
Cold piece of toast chewed by dogs
And in the morning sun baked broken glass
Shards below slate
Awaiting release shine
Like beacons to the assembled world.

Radio

1

Turn the radio on: a sub-text
of adjacent planes abutted
against each other, pushing
like continental plates & breaking
free of context; dark low clouds
counterpointing white narcissus.

Turn the radio off; discover the beach
is on the roof. Dust falls in one hell
of an electric glow, hits the
terminal jetty. The riveters have
fixed the yellow warning
notice to the wire fence:

it has no message for you. Turn the TV
on, reminisce about the 60s,
you could almost feel history
coming through between your fingers,
a bit iffy, just like a child who
commences to sing

"You make me feel brand new
You make me feel so clean right through"
"Don't say such things dear Papa
I'm home again and I'm so happy"
Turn the TV off buy a clean shirt
put it on. That was the 60s.

2

Recurrence & difference; it's all there is.
And I have built this house of cards;
it is personal & has taken
a considerable amount of effort

to make glamorous
& particular, full of the presence

of the 4-minute warning, of
words spoken
by the girl & her detective friend
going into unexplored territory
in search of a sub-text. Turn the radio on
Interference from cars from

concrete shields random noise
not screened, signal fluctuates like
film noir without the vision.
Between the spectrum & the code
words spoken fly towards the Pleiades.

They fly towards heat death, & we
shall walk upon the beach
together. The white narcissus
in the breadbin, the falling dust.
It's less than a dream
but more than a conclusion.

Total Allergy Syndrome

I am cured of the past but I know it very well –Pierre Boulez

Man points pistol between woman's parted
thighs pointing upward thighs frame the composition
a mimetic dance that issues in revolt
the difference is organised collectively
evoked & expelled to reveal its name they impinge
cast their shadows before staff or wand substitute
but its lustre spread   guns falling   lips of the
language class raised to a higher power

Mediated very precisely   keep yer lip buttoned up
strict time sequenced in any order
each picture is like a labyrinth
half electronic & really kind of half human
screen glows then flashes staccato the beats
are not real beats but cues
legato staccato articulation of wrists
songs of dogs & transistors you yourself are the sign

The towers the contingent necessities
the darkness touched flesh of your arms
& face no burning screen illuminated the towers
the edge of dread the images of desire
at the perimeter new weather systems
ruptured the contingent necessities   the pistol
the edge of dread   video galaxies multiply desire
red-shifted into the heat zone the darkness

Mediated by contingent necessities   the towers
frame the composition a mimetic dance
at the perimeter encircled fast
about & drifting white water like stars
half human screen glows   the towers & behind them
the towers falling darkness breathing
vast company decoding ten million events
when only five or six are significant

Lip palate scaled cold fence wire
thighs pointing upward desire red-shifted
into dread galaxies   flesh pulsing "brighter
than a thousand suns" accelerating from the towers
at 9.80665 metres per second per second
but I will make a trial of love per second per second
red-shifted into a safe margin
a describable structure a place of sanctuary

Rules are suspended   connections severed   body earthed
in the afterglow behind the towers
lips expel air into the darkness the lustre
into the main event   into the singularity
of a nation   of staff or wand substitute
to reveal its name its contingent necessities
fit face to memory   thighs to wrists
lip to palate at the perimeter

I think I'm made of this type of wood
20th century is almost not touched
the beats are not real beats the towers are the towers
you yourself are the sign the stigmata
she bears desire that does not name or frame
the edge of dread the end of night
what would it be like for this
poem to have a use   this is done very quickly

Listen to Britain

She told us she was never well
– on her white cheeks
down which the tidal ditch continues
its course the air is loaded: "I have 2 brains & they're not
speaking to one another." We
learn that names are important
at this time, & about then she was put away
with sunk eyes, with the dark
areolae around, where biochemistry

meets cybernetics chemical chord
sparked head turned to light
nuclear jewels in relation to
society; it *was* inadmissible. Like
tins in which the 78 needles had
mental pictures that went with the words
with many rooms, each phrase of the
father had the same mental pictures too,
would admit of being
mapped out pathologically.

The derelict house, windows grimy &
half boarded, 3 storeys up he
flicks on ceefax slackens back &
the train moves on, down the long
tunnel it's a bullet
in a gun it's a bulletin. He sits
leant forward head cupped in one hand
between the knees. And all around him
a belt of bullets
set in crooked slates, through which

pigeons fly to nest
from the reeking leather-dresser's
mumbling poetry spontaneously
generated language, particularly

that didn't make sense & the whole thing
in relation to authoritarian
lumpers engaged in discharging
no distinction between
artificial systems &
living systems mining an oppressive

world, which is no bloody good,
was disturbed because they
used to stand on the bed jumping with
risk shipping the fossils,
names of your own choosing, which they do.
A choice could be repress a wish to
transgress these restrictions or tear
the web clearly & understand when & where
the wealth flowing from London's commerce
used to do that too, but that was when we

learnt the "real" word "music" (though
conversations at the bus stop
invade dreams before morning,
sliding through a clear space through
impaired digestion languid circulation
saturated with the very excrements
of their fellow creatures who invented the
word for Music). Move off the streets
the heart of a nation
& you move into the silence,

cherry red with a picture of the HMV dog.
It waits to be ruptured, in a generous
way, no chance through the
radio years to do something with
language that is at bottom an individual
but not a private speech
(even when you are attacking or under
amused by it) & it was necessary for
socialisation, being made to understand
a church, a kind of dim blue-lit building.

Weapons Systems – Version I

Windows tinted with pure gold to keep out glare, composite video signals. All decisions are recorded on tape for analysis by game control. Confronting suffering and evil, a machine that lets the morbid brain talk. They can build you an accelerator to do everything. An electric field which holds the particle beam very closely to the axis. The memory problem is a major snag. The imagined sympathy of fishes; glean from them the moral slant. And now: a choice of viewing. Should provide an exceptional listening experience when heard on any high quality playback or broadcast system. Where was gravity before Newton discovered it? A man in a white coat appears carrying what looks like a giant rusty beach ball. What it amounts to is that you are faced with a succession of binary choices. Vigilance was to be maintained at programme, not management level. When you type one line, an automatic censor comes into operation. An uncooperative target, which is very shiny, which is very fast, would be extremely difficult to hit. Eight corporations dominate American weapon production. One microscopic flaw, and some of that energy would be absorbed. They drove the cattle into a pit. Rarely seen, they gain in moral stature every time their absence is mentioned. The eating of human flesh as a source of horror. The story is tragic in its later implications of tortured silence. Each unit contains the code for the whole. Polar bear only £2.50. Combines a crafty design with total simplicity. The secret is real dairy butter. There's a special chapter in the manual on all this. The implications of being able to take a critical view of what had hitherto been transitory were not good. The graphics system teaches you new thought styles. We just have to ask the Generals to be good boys. If you miss, there is nothing to tell you how far off target you were. When Avon is captured by punitive warriors and Vila discovers that the silo containing Scorpio is impossible to open, it looks as though things cannot get any worse for the survivors of the Liberator. This is an ingenious idea, but becomes wearisome after an extremely short space of time. Among them was a resurgence of the old Romantic ideal of limitless individual potential. Excited by a powerful electric discharge, weight for weight one of the toughest weapons in existence. The new grammar begins to invade your conversation. They become more complex until they reach the point where they begin to break down. The clinic pays my wages; I'm just a PE instructor. The market is where the action is; the poachers are the best regulators. Put space mirrors near these accelerators. Soldiers in suspended cages, horse had its throat cut while it stood in its stable, prisoner threw himself about his cell in a fit of madness. Could science help us make sense of such a world? Thieves broke in and made off with 29 valuable reptiles. It is all a matter of feedback loops, cloud seeding to make rain, insertion of cloned genes for the ozone of a competitive life, probably fear. These men would have to kneel here for about 2 months before they keeled over. One would have thought with the excessive casualty figures that shoes would have been extremely plentiful. This is how dreams begin. Men in hats shot them. If the language is suspect, then invent a new language. Send no money now. Designer's knowledge of polymers. This column of air. This is the mouse the cat the dog the man the car knocked down beat chased ate.

Shadow of White Days

(for Allen Fisber)

Frequency
                                        And Amplitude
You can't hold down the line your body
malfunctions. The shadow of white days.

First   there was silence
and then
there was silence.
(Refrigerator hums   clock ticks)

"At the Elephant & Castle
even people
will disintegrate"
(Original signal was a moon echo)

Turn / in the light
It is time
Best before date shown,
do not re-freeze.

Attack, decay
timbre, frequency & amplitude
And then silence, the fugue
comes to an end.

Loss of, loss of
Angry tears flood
visible surface stretched from code to code
essence of thought.

Your body in the light
of the bright video screen
signals across galaxies
Moving from one room to the next

Change
        It is time
"What does not change"
the art of fugue

Shadow
creeps across the allotment
into any community
creeps.

Dogs behind wire,
radio
        on. Words into phonemes
blips speed up.

Women at the wire
        change the meaning
of the body, move outward
from silence.

Change / what does not change
Best before date shown before &
after silence. Change bodies, change heart
change art, the shadow of white days.

Wall of Silence in Chinatown

(to Louis Zukofsky)

Flakes of your lips
move down to the street falling

like early snow that
vanishes in the runnels.

Emotions – or their empty form
or the effect of them

in a distant country friends
have led you through. The cathedral

dome's illuminated
by floodlight behind a grid

of silence; endless
night beyond that again

fills vision, erasing
lines one by one, it's like

a video of the Dungeness hum.
What magic against that what

heliotrope to wear as you
enter its magnetosphere as

snow slowly or rapidly
fills the screen? Empty form –

not melodious but with the effect
of melody. You are not That.

Hoping This Scribble Finds You Still Well As It Leaves Me Just Ordinary

(4 postcards from the perimeter – for Julia Phillips)

1

Victory Community Park.
No Dogs. No Cycling.
Ball Games only in Sunken Play Area.
Equipment used at your Own Risk.
Please use Litter Bins.
Don't climb Perimeter Fence.

2

Don't
Mind's a blank
Without
Write it down
Forget it if you don't
Get it all down

3

7 Kings: discarded wood & rubble

flat rainswept landscape

4

They painted the wall the
wrong green, he said,
anger tensing his body
momentarily.

A feeling of desolation
And white clouds
Breaking

Was that Harry
He must have thought I was a
complete idiot.

Parabola / Perimeter

You perceive the images
& despite the fact that

everything has happened twice before
nothing is familiar;

four out of ten for appearance.
Money speaks to you

but its utterances are mere ritual
for coping with doubt: "I am easy

& nice." "Mark time." 15 years later
you're still walking down the same street.

You live dangling.
Production explodes.

You're driving through the rush-hour. Suddenly
you are pistol-whipped into oblivion,

It's looking quite good
rupturing both liver & diaphragm;

It is almost always
not what you wanted.

Hungry like the Wolf.
Hungry for love.

Hungry like video to video.
Certainly; mitten on a crisp.

It's like being armlocked by 2
policemen into a new

& mysterious neighbourhood.
It certainly makes you think.

You want to be loved yet
you are always crashing into the furniture.

And this cannot but signify
that your exclusion is really from power – the

mummy & daddy of a money explosion.
And this cannot be

the meaning encoded within the message
& it is this realisation that induces

sweat gland secretion & generally
makes life difficult with its promise

of fullness that is never delivered.
You walk into a room &

then you walk into a wall.
You'll never get there.

You're too
hungry for contradiction.

You face the music
& the music faces you.

You know this picture quite well
but you cannot describe it.

Five Nocturnes, After Derek Jarman

1

About this time streetlamps flicker up like
Work of art in an age of mechanical reproduction,
Pink pin pricks slowly flower pink to gold glare.
All of a sudden Baby starts to speak fluent german,
A man & his dog become shadow of a man & his dog
Spontaneously everything is terrifically brilliant.
Each evening takes a photograph each evening
Becomes lighter; worm of power grows.

Gold burns in lightbulb egg or golden apple
Burns in satin now that's ruined your day.
Very important lots of money
No information at all flowers bloom sodium
Fuels brilliant sunsets seen behind protective glass.
Bang bang shoot shoot in every art gallery.

2

An art of definition – is this
– surface of hand on surface (boundary)
Of glass? or is it "I intend to jump
Off this ledge & get happy"?

Writing unwrites itself into
Chance encounters configurations
That are politically indeterminate like rubber
Ball trajectories in a confined

Space; but an art of definition; at what
Point does the ink itself begin to
Speak what does it say

Why want to make time stand still?
Between lightbulb & the idea of lightbulb
Falls the shadow.

3

This juxtaposition of events without
Perspective: chinese mat, magazines, ash-tray,
Concord sonata 1st american in space.
On a glass table the objects, held
By the circle that bounds them,
Struggle to break free of the authoritarian
Figure, with its connotation
Of repeating, & the idea of a centre.

So you keep hanging onto the appearances
How they might be saved by epicycle
Upon epicycle in the comforting dark
When sodium flare reveals those orbits
Twin focussed, not as they might be,
Ineluctably tousled as they are.

4

De – um majorettes
Doin' mah writin
Clear light evening
Goes down slowly

Not finished – not yet
Who is responsible for these
Black silhouettes
A magic zone a protected zone

Became the laziest 8th king
2 goats pandas crabs & a friesian bull
What's the connection

Buy emphasizers, cow gum, album for art work
New FT index
Will blow your mind

5

Night falls on single vision zombies everywhere
O that lonely Feb. moon in a clear sky
Occasionally perceived between the flats is it
(a) mythopoeic construct (b) collage?

If there's an answer there must be a
Question (Gertrude Stein). Write the essentials only.
Moonlight on wilting
                    Spider plant, make

Shadows
                    Gone
Whirling through stages of a spiral blood game

Nights in the city. so pretty. so
Slovenly, lovely. all of us here
Breathing out. breathing in. breathing out

Banknotes That Made History
(Weapons Systems – Version 2)

Gold sprayed spanners were used as give-aways, and a 16-ft version was used as the centre-piece. The biting weather throughout February seemed to numb my brain – it certainly gave me two lovely colds which hung on and on, but enough of me. Every possible ounce of benefit was squeezed out of rock made to resemble a piece of copper tube. Every inch of ground had to be fought for aggressively. The age of the plastic daffodils is gone: 150 people all wanting to stub their fag ends out on the carpets and table tops.

We made £41 at the last jumble sale. Can one be of science or a politician coincident in democracy with some others if one is afraid to be known to support constant value and even the principle that legal tender remain the award it was inferred to be as certificate of good labour? Pam (No. 10) has a coal bunker outside her front door which she wants to get rid of – any takers? I've got a 4-ft white wrought iron headboard to sell for £1. The uniqueness of these products explains their popularity as self-liquidators. And the other predominant emblem is the English rose. I'll look out for cheap red white and blue crepe paper and anything else we can use.

Leaving out much that it may be thought is by an aggregately humble consumer as I expressible about office of indeterminate privilege, liability and inhumanity, labour, time, paper, etc, waste and to even more expediently than is otherwise possible describe an advanced state of civilized democracy, I hereunder infer such state operative. "Meet the Soft Machine, says Mary Quant." He saw a clear opportunity with our sunglasses. As a number of men in high places will vouch, steel girders had been passed on repeatedly, to widen awareness of the code, blowing a trumpet, but signifying little or nothing. It is that no longer by feudal habit do our Local Councillors seem inferred village idiots, and now that we have almost full participation by the electorate at local elections quite other. We now have a different liaison officer, Mr Phil Collins, if we need guidance on anything, but basically we're running the show. Positions may well stiffen; change in attitude and in behaviour is still necessary in the public interest; the design, implementation and control of programmes seeking to increase the acceptability of a social idea, cause or practice made me feel quite mean.

Although a difficult value-system problem, the manipulation of pleasure and pain to bring about change makes the desired behaviour almost unrefusable. Doreen Russell suggested a theme of feathers. Pick a

Perfect Husband; Win Tomorrow's World. Now upon the coincidence of a formal vote of Councillors throughout Britain with one of two proposed schedules (pro deflation), (pro speculator), incomes and expenditures of the public treasury are authorised. The canned steam even penetrated the Iron Curtain, where personality girls were used because they infringe the basic rules. A paradise of humming birds and sugar birds making people redundant, a high degree of flexibility in a cold economic climate, with flexible use among the sexes, a system of demountable or telescopic ramped benches to give maximum flexibility; the memories are still fresh. It may very well have not been possible for this state of peace and fuller democracy to have been reached ever.

The Great Tradition

(to David Jones)

1

Logic proportion & coherence
tattoo'd on a
shaven skull

Was a very patriarch

BEING on one bicep
BECOMING on the other

•

I see a space I see chimney rubble
matière stuff, not subject,
I and I.   Who
is this I that speaks etc.
The dreadful night is over I see
white clouds breaking
signs ruptured
                                        at the edge of
                                        what happened.

•

Read how they refused
to unload the copper
And how the people were
Strong

The rims are between our fingers
And the circles
Tokens of love, logic
proportion & coherence

and we raise them to our
lips & share this
dancing light. And who
are we now that do this?

•

It is not a conduit
nor a vessel.

•

Read about the dockers in
burnished glory, dispossessed
like foxes & adders
by the move downriver,
and the watermen, no wherries now in
twin screw diesel tugs
equipped with Voith-Schneider propulsion,

how the men's bitterness
overflowed, the long ago fathers
and the long ago mothers
of us all, chained
to the bottom of the boat, strike
Lord Devonport dead, or else
it's the hulks & the Spike

or you swallowed the anchor –
hard morsel – in sweat shops &
steam
          in Marshalsea Rd   in Borough High St
under the arches at Charing X, or broke
stones for the Governor,
milled them to bits could make
no human design of it.

•

And clustered in groups
for survival   came
through the loopholes
at
            Butler's Wharf
            Hay's Wharf
            Gun & Shot Wharves
                                                  "the dream
has the structure of a sentence
or rather   of a rebus.
But even this   "

expressing itself at some points
as action, at others only when
having disengaged the deep structure, the
idea of a history of the objects
or of the surface phenomena
has been replaced,   perpetuates
an illusion.

•

A range of habitats
scrub, grassland a pond
has been established   a wide variety
of invertebrates
in a derelict lorry park
"it seemed only natural".

It is a trace
It is the trace of a presence it is We

Every truth
                        is a partial truth.

•

The thought in my mouth
Because speaking is magic

And I carried this with me
But the language has shifted
Would not tell me
what I wanted to know.

Could not swallow this no
longer down the little red lane;
walked up Gt Dover St near Guy's
through stink of bridges, skirt pool
in the subway, an operative
paradigm, saturated.

Explored the sense the tension
dispersed through spinal column
vertical through th'occipital
cavity. They came through the loopholes,
passed amid hearty cheers. They
must be strong if they are to move
not from song, rather
from discourse.

•

They are the sins of the fathers
visited onto the sons.

And diversity is come
out of unity.
Out of the heart of a nation.

Was a very patriarch
lost in the mesh
ribbed mud
his broken speech
behind the estates
tattoo removal by laser
this is war
in the magnetosphere

•

The rims are between our fingers
And the circles

Your head held in the vortex
your feet in flux.

At the edge of what happened.

•••

2

Logic proportion & coherence
were crossing a bridge
between the known bank &
the unknown.

And below the bridge
lived

but that
is another story.

Envoi

You're looking at the dashboard of the new Ford Sierra
please do not formulate
a critique of would be reassuring deceptions
or their labyrinthine financial arrangements.
Thank you.

You are looking at where home
used to be   at wallpaper exposed to wind & rain
too late for that I'm afraid
pigeons flock & fly around the houses once.

Behind every gleaming exterior
there is a classic struggle for survival
in a variety of habitats   not one of them
without its invisible perimeter.
Signs ruptured, cold flags flicker vehicles
cruising into the zone.

This is a car for the eighties
it has an acoustic sandwich floor
man & machine in perfect rupture   rapture
Thank you so much.

You're looking at the age of the train
& the brain & the rain & the pain & the drain
& the video age too – yummy –
it's wedge shaped it's aerodynamically something
special in the yellow smoke that hangs about anyhow.

So mind how you go.

A4 Portrait

1984

Part 1: approaching

13. ix. 83
Where there is light
And the people are kind
Small pebbles held in the hand
Pleasingly textured white
And it's quiet
Except for   & between   & beyond
Stars appear then
Vega – in the lyre
I have changed
26 light years
Nights days will come & go
Astonishingly
Circles
Seen only at a distance the energy
Returns
From fragment to whole
And back
Falling into space a vortex
A coffee cup
With the brown ring in the bottom
Rests on a wooden
Table where there is light

13. ix. 83
Drive along the road
From point A to point A^1
Fog descends & spreads
Lights appear shimmer colours beyond
15 years have gone by
News comes on the radio
A continuing pattern a trace
Of archaic voices
Interference pattern a handshake for the cameras
Light refracted in every direction
No coherence to it wet windy weather

Approaching from the west
From east from south & north
The road returns
A mystery
How it appears

14. ix. 83
Maybe this is right
Maybe we should go this way look
It's happened again
Tomorrow these people will go home
And it will be quiet
Today we got stuck in the woods
We scratched our hands & faces
Looking for a way out in the
Rain that starts to fall
A dog comes to show us the way
To guard us
Good dog
Anyway
What were we talking about
Let's not talk about it any more
It's still raining
I am certain of this
At least I was
We walk & walk
Presently we shall come to our destination

16. ix. 83
Approaching … approaching …
Round the corner
Is the bridge
It goes on forever over the river
White sun shines
On the ripples I feel a vague deep feeling
The doors open on their own
Cloud hides the sun we're back to the
Beginning

Ripples of light
Hugging the trucks
Face in the glass where are we
Superimposed
And the curves are quite pleasing
How they run into one another
Now it's dark
The radio plays the animals
Move slowly in the shadow
Where are we now
Approaching

Part 2: getting there

17. ix. 83
The key is on the table
But she did
Not turn up
And now it's all down to waiting
And it'll come out in the wash
But I wish you hadn't said that
We surely can't have been right
Eight of us, & six of us
On time
Drinking wine
Etc.
Home & get some sleep oh well
Always an adjunct
A vortex
Between the individual desire
And the impinging realities
Got to work tomorrow
Very low key, laid
Back, sort of
Chronological I mean
Gaps between to be filled
To be sure but OK
Very much as before
Once more
With feeling with holding with very
Best wishes
Love, & you seal the envelope
It does not have
Far to go
You feel much better about things it
Shows

20. ix. 83
The mother stands with hands in pockets
The child kicks the ball
In a fenced off area in a space
Below & to the right
Isobars deck the prognosis
Settle into a rhythm
That feels comfortable & at the same time
A column of air breathed in
Breathed up
And exhaled upon
Currents that circulate
In a nexus
A frontal awareness a sort of opposite
Of a vortex
Ping-pong ball on the jet
Always in motion & always there
And suddenly the mother is gone
The child
A loved one disappears up the lane
Wearing blue shoes
Nothing is as it was before
The rhythm
Starts to break up in a space
That is determined by where it's going
Which is a point in a fabric
Of uncertainty
The child walked on the pebbles
Insistently
The wind blew on the roof
You are a breath away the beat
Of a heart
From the not yet verified
Moving from nowhere to somewhere
In time & out of time

22. ix. 83
The mistakes are not miracles
The road leads to here
He sees but does not understand
He does not see the mistakes
This is information
Of which he is unaware
He does not hear the road
He hears the road but does not understand
Where it leads
The road leads to information
And if the breath
And if the supply
Should fail
You having trouble with that door
I'm not going anywhere
Not yet

24. ix. 83
Parked cars
In a half light
Delineate an absence or the
Boundary of one
And sometimes you may find yourself
Here
Once again
And the question then is
How did you get here & is there
Adequate means of escape
And the thought passes
A loved one approaches
Same as the day before & the
Day before that
Time for lunch
At the event horizon
Five cars parked
No Entry One Way
And sometimes

There is no mistake the wind
Abates
It's quiet
Five cars
One arrives with the loved one
The loved one arrives
Twenty minutes late
What am I doing here
Approaching
10 to 3
Some of the answers are right
Some are wrong
You have no way of knowing
And there's not much time left
Surely this time
we'll find out

25. ix. 83
Where is the loved one going
Sugar on a glass table
Splits the light
Returns
The quiet suddenly broken
The curve
She's much happier there
She won't talk about it
Triangulation of the 4 corners
I wish you hadn't come
Get up move slowly
Across the room, a coffee cup
Gleams
No coherence to it
No way of analysing
The play
A knock on the door
And everything changes again
Without warning

26. ix. 83
Fireworks
A warm night
The sky opens out
Like a flower
Nobody around
Water flows
Out of the tap
"It was believed
They had created a real
But incomprehensible
Language"

27. ix. 83
This one looks
As though it's going to be oh
what comes next
How does it go I know
It had to be seen to be believed
A real dog's breakfast
Every discursive account
Every discursive account
Every discursive account
Is a betrayal
(*Bernard Noël*)
Toasting
Despairs yet chooses
Despairs yet chooses
Not concerned with relating
But with awakening
Breakfast
Yes please
Awe inspiring really

28. ix. 83
There are fingers
Holding a pen pushing & pulling it
Across a somewhat narrow page

They come to a stop
Here there is a blank
Then start again
Anything can be a stimulus
Forget what the last line was
Start again from the blank
The point however is to keep going
Clinging to the page
Like a mountaineer on a sheer face
The point however is to fall off
That is
Lose control
And then it becomes interesting
So long as you
So long as you what
Right we're at the bottom now
So turn the page
Now I definitely can't see my past
How did they know how to stop
And start again just there
The musicians I mean
"Gingerbread, Gingerbread Boy"
(*Archie Shepp*)
The activity
Itself
External to this is something else
Now it becomes interesting
There's a natural motion to it
Textural nuances or something
I mean you know when it stops
And it hasn't yet
And you go into phrases
Read off from a whole life support system
Stuff like
But ultimately this is a diversion
A distraction from
The business itself
The fingers the pen the motor skills
Somehow in communication with a brain

And the whole co-ordinated by some kind
of energy system
Or not as the case may be
And standing in certain relationships
No cross that out put in
But the rules don't permit it
What rules
What rules do you mean

30. ix. 83
Siren in the night
A rise & fall
Somewhere
Everything is laid bare
Never a silent one
3 of us in the room
This dynamic
Such accuracy
Such a long time ago
You don't remember do you
Stomach pain
The girl got better
But it's too late she was
Never the same
Now a quick noise
Then that fades too
In the night in the unseen distance

2. x. 83
"I want to bring the
Void to life"
(*Franju*)
The closed window
Playing the old tunes
The partly closed window
The open window
Do it quickly
Not with but through

Or was it the other way round
Now comes the hard part
Heartbeat faster
Subjective
Like a distorting mirror
There are ways & means
(Enumerate)
When the light's on, the
Window's a mirror

3. x. 83
But what's subjective
What reduction
There's no distinction
Possible
Men & women the world
The magnetic network that
Holds it together
Shockwave from a solar flare
Caused auroral displays
Wrought havoc with short-wave radio
Blood & brine
Maintain course
Struggle to be defined as subjects
In their own lives
But what are subjects
If not subjected objects
Forget it
The loved one returns
Siren returns
Here
Information returns
Because the people the ripples
The sun
Return
Remember it shining through the bridge
A door shuts
Quietly

5. x. 83
There's no question about it
No room for discussion
All to no avail
Three people arrive
Unexpectedly, i.e.
They are not the ones you expected
There have been some changes
A cat leaps under the
Glass table
Everyone comes to the same
Conclusion
It's exciting being at the corner
Because you have 2 edges
And you feel you're really *at* the edge
And then there's a whole page
About the year ahead of you
Except that's someone else
The cat starts to wash its paws
They went out with the stated intention of
Getting drunk
This could be a
Crucial day in your life
And you'd never know

6. x. 83
Something's happening
A conversation
Without resolution
Unmapped
In good faith
You can't ask for more
And the perception of it
Which is editing
As you go along so to speak
It's slow here
You walk from one end of the room
To the other

You walk into the bar
It's early evening
But the sun's gone down
And you catch some dialogue
Unexpectedly
Which is instantly replayed
And subjected to analysis
A man who is powerful
Becomes a victim
A reporter in the stadium
Comes from another, bluish world
The image does not shimmer
But glows in the dusk
Some people want it all
Done for them
Because it's always been done for them
And something's dying
But you don't want to think about that
Not now
Not when you've come this far

7. x. 83
Show a person a picture
And a word appears
Now there's another
They are objects
Now living under assumed names
Sublunar
And therefore mutable
The dance I am doing is an obscure dance
This can't be right
And yet And yet
Images are saturated
Colours bleed
A band of blue across the eyes
I was a subject in mathematical arrangements
Now the spool unspools
Clever of you to think of that

Persistence of vision that
Laminates the retina
Fuses past to future
In a broth of present a magnetic
Soup in other words
Power bleeds through the visible spectrum
It's got a hold on you
It's fascination
Polarity
Potential difference
Search for a relation
That is not a spark out of this
And you search in vain
The past & the future
You & me
You get the picture
You're *in* the picture
So how do you get from one frame
To the next
This is a sorry state of affairs
Power sparks 24 times per second
Somebody called it truth
That's really funny
I am in one picture you're in the next
Shot
Reverse shot
When in doubt
Have a man enter the room
With a signifier in his hand
Power & love
The 2 edges
(*Rainer Werner Fassbinder, b. 1946, d. 1982*)

7. x. 83
You can't just
Make up a language
You have to work
With what you've got

But you can make it
Different
A hand repeatedly
Fails to grasp a bouquet

Devon – London

A4 Landscape

1988

September 1984: Yorkshire Dales

The sun shines on the dull snout of the retreating glacier.
Contour lines call to one another from great distances.
Glacial drift spreads nourishment from the Silurian layers.
Thistledown gathers radio space.

Somehow, broken wire frames a sheep in lamb.
The sound of an enigma breaks the stillness.
A greeting is precious beyond all estimation.
Time is congealed & unable to circulate among meadows.

Sheep challenge visual perception.
A dead bird is "of the essence".
On the thread of a distant road, is hung a grey shirt.
To follow the line is to lose that lamb.

Steam condenses on the window beside corrugated iron.
I took a deep breath, and suddenly the room seemed filled.

"The more of life you include the more unstable the problem."

17 March 84
Pub upper room / large, cold posters of folk
Screen for slide projection cassette player
Clive had bluetacked long computer printouts
To the mantelpiece dark except for side lamp
Use of old book tape fades out
Lapsing into pure voice sound in response
From time to time
Length of performance: hard to judge

18 April 84
An eerie silence has settled over the area
Police marksmen hold their positions
The only people left are journalists
Leaders of the miners' union are meeting tonight
From Sheffield our industrial correspondent
Cloudy in London overnight, with just the odd spot of rain

27 April 84
All day
The destination & route of the Libyans remained a mystery
Eight wardrobes full of pineapples
Lovely

28 April 84
5 pigeons on roof, 2 on parapet
Male strut (courtship) green neck puffed tip
12.07: 2 more join the group ranged on raked slates
5 fly in the air a short distance settle again after a moment
12.09: Now 11 in total all on the roof
4 of lighter body with dark barred wings, 2 self groom
13.01: No pigeons

29 April 84
Sea still very cold, general synopsis at 1900 low west Shannon
Complex low Spain moving slow east. No change
Cromarty Forth southerly 6 perhaps increasing gale 8 later

Fair, moderate or good
Blonde, sanguine, in clinch with Irishman in bow tie
German Bight: locally 4 easterly 5 in south
Biscay: easterly 6 decreasing 4 or 5 in north
Showers, moderate or good
Quality homes, traditionally built. Quality homes of character.
Lundy Fastnet: south easterly 4 or 5 increasing 6
Locally 7, rain in south east later, good
Shannon Rockall: mainly south easterly, becoming cyclonic
Occasional rain, moderate or good
Gas fired central heating, luxury fitted kitchens & bathrooms
Scilly east 5, 9 miles, 1,012, falling slowly
Jersey east 4, 13 miles, 1,013, rising more slowly
From Mull of Galloway to Berwick upon Tweed
An anticyclone near Jutland will decline slowly
While depression increases over England

5 May 84
Death threats to sheep
Belonging to Britain's leading Catholic family

12 May 84
Patchy cloud in the south of the country
A steady fall of pressure over the British Isles
Pleasure points plotted Lundy Fastnet north east 4
Locally 5 in south: fair, good.
"That feeling of tantalising uncertainty."
Hebrides south west 4 or 5 increasing 6 or 7
Moderate with fog patches, becoming good later
"There is nothing that we exclude from our work."
Malin Head south east by south 4, 22 miles, 1,022
Rising more slowly. "The Eye sees more than the Heart knows."

April 1985:
Elephant & Castle, London

Large spaces in the shopping mall; a boy,
A gun, & a pretty ugly dog. The circuitry
Is quite complicated and all of the
Trees in the park are in blossom; the speed
Of writing being unpredictable, there is no
Way of telling how the next moment might shape.
For example: Pressure will be high to the
North-west of Ireland, maintaining a rather
Cold north or north-easterly flow
Over the British Isles; the morning light
Will be unevenly distributed over the wire
Cages; these are the words; no-one will own them.

This note is to tell you that payment
Of your unemployment benefit, apart from any
Payment on its way to you, has been suspended
While a decision is made about your claim.

Trees in the park are in blossom; the speed
Is quite complicated and all of the
Circuitry the. dog ugly pretty a &, gun a,
Boy a; mall shopping the in spaces large.
This note is to tell you, these are the words
Of your unemployment benefit, apart from any
Way of telling how the next moment might shape.
Payment, on its way to you, has been suspended.
For example: a gun, & a pretty ugly dog.
For example: no-one will own them.
For example: the morning light. Large spaces
Will be unevenly distributed over the wire.

These are the words. And these
Are the meanings of the words.
These are the words.
And these are the meanings of the words.

13 May 84
Fenchurch Street, Barking, Upminster, West Horndon, Laindon,
Basildon, Pitsea, Benfleet for Canvey Island, Leigh-on-Sea

19 May 84
6.33 pm: 5 pigeons on roof one white one
2 on parapet copulate briefly then remain together
Female grooming: light haze, warm

23 May 84
"I was body popping in St John's Wood I have been
moved on by the police that's a true story."
"Good evening, this is Orson Welles." Qu'est-ce qu'il a dit?
A new chair, a new typewriter, a new start
The hero of the hour

30 May 84
"We're in this wonderful theatre and the singing of the birds
Accompanies our talk."

6 June 84
"England over increases depression while slowly
Decline will Jutland near anticyclone an slowly
More rising, 1,013, miles 13, east 4 Jersey slowly falling"
"Cold very still sea" "parapet on 2, roof on pigeons 5"

7 June 84
Miners in town today in red & yellow caps
Boy gets off & on a bus, distributes papers to
Passers by. Cardigan tied around the waist.
Blaze of sun its power a million years hence

4 July 84
An anticyclone is centred over the UK & will drift slowly east
Fair, visibility good, becoming moderate towards dawn
No silence soft through vibrates dead pigeon
Heat through moving flux metallic blue towards dawn disclosing

7 July 84
Towards moderate becoming, good visibility, fair

8 September 84
White light at the edge of night hard
Wide circle all around a mesh of resistance
Secret electricity, steel & contaminated meat

10 September 84
White stains the edge of serrated leaf forms
A flock of pigeons and then a single pigeon
A single pigeon and then no pigeon at all

22 October 84
Rain at first, but becoming dry with sunny intervals
developing. Wind NW, moderate. Near normal.
Sunny periods, isolated showers developing. Wind W or NW,
moderate. Near normal.
Sunny intervals and scattered showers. Wind W to NW,
moderate or fresh. Near normal.
Rather cloudy with showers, perhaps heavy and prolonged
in places. Wind W, strong. Near normal.

26 November 84
Nine months of the miners' strike
Sounds in the night & lights in the sky

July 1985:
Winster ➲ Derby via Sheffield (for Tony & Liz)

Shining Cliff Woods: sound of water begins to impinge
Smaller & more powerful than anything imagined.
On the opposite bank a dragonfly escapes rain
Filters through the beech its yellow sheath.

People are bringing food out to eat in the garden
When suddenly the clarity of the air extends
To the distant workings; colour transforms the village
Into a torrent, or a dissonance.

In the studio, big pictures of people rearranged
To suit circumstances & Japanese paper money
Placed at intervals grind their teeth in sleep . . .
The distant city lights up like a flare.

A Christ made of vegetables & a powder blue sky
Unfilled-in, permutations so very un-English
Confuse pastoral hardboard, cricket, salad greenfly
And a huge graveyard with the urns half draped.

Then along the rail sparrows jump fluffy
Beside engineering works nipping the wrong half.
Looking forward to or gathered that it would just
Take too long, move the writing by hops on.

And in the secret pool that afternoon a fish leaps
For a moment to make the air more silver
As it shimmers towards an undetermined affinity
Outside of all shadows.

23 December 84
Car hits a pile of sand too fast
Comes off the road, hits tree & parked car
Everything's rearranged, no loss of nerve, no blame

24 December 84
Waterloo, Vauxhall, Clapham Junction, Earlsfield, Wimbledon,
Raynes Park, New Malden, Norbiton, Kingston

26 December 84
Kingston, Norbiton, New Malden, Raynes Park, Wimbledon,
Earlsfield, Clapham Junction, Vauxhall, Waterloo

28 December 84
Fog begins to envelop the mysterious building
He is trapped into repeating the same actions
Over again – as though this were something
He had no part in making

6 January 85
Flight of pigeons in a dark window
First snow of the winter falls
New technology destroys 55% of jobs in the mining industry
On TV a trawler cuts through Indian fishermen's nets
Ice making factory families grow rich
Frozen prawns in polythene

9 January 85
Flight of pigeons cuts through Indian fishermen's nets
On TV ice making factory families grow rich
Frozen prawns in a dark window, the winter

19 January 85
"He felt no sensation. Only in the last few moments
does he realise what has occurred."
The railway runs alongside the building
Geraldine gave way to Gilbert, with Maggie doing movement
Spotlamp too bright, space too cold
A telephone rings somewhere in the building
Lose the focus

25 January 85
Sees a young tree with wire surrounding
Tape recorder, razor blades, secret programme of the Lyric Suite
Interferes with miners' strike via the stratosphere
Integrated & closer to the tonality fragmented

3 February 85
"Listen to Britain" Planes in formation
Dancers Train   Factory
Signal against night sky   "The Ash Grove"
Big Ben Bicycles at the factory gate
Power station, trees, children, photographs
Steelworks in the sky   Rule Britannia
Power station & cornfields, clouds

7 February 85
"For each of the events listed, try to think of a specific event
or experience – the day, place & circumstances, if possible."
"Virtues & vices become civic rather than tragic & individual."
"Select five words that best describe you."
(Afraid   Creative   Emotional   Intelligent   Misunderstood)
"And literature shifts from its concern for the relationship
between God and man to a concern for the relationship between
man and society."
"Write any additional words if the above list is not descriptive
enough to reflect your true feelings."

September 1985:
Deserted mills, Oldham, Lancs

Rose/pink mills blur in a haze of morning fog
As a fire prevention truck swivels into the empty yard
One magpie for sorrow, a man & his dog, a wet meadow decay
Among new brick, a show of strength

Seven miles from the Arndale Centre a seagull screams, the traffic doesn't stop
Dog leaps, red clover scatters, a baby is born
Sun burns through the haze & honey scent warms jogger's limbs
Articulating left to right then right to left

After seven days another baby's born again from rubble
What mean spirit could survive such golden slumbers
Ten past 11 Sunday morning, the cries of children on the breeze their shadows
Begin to dance across the meadow

10 February 85
Victoria, Denmark Hill, Peckham Rye, Crofton Park, Catford,
St Mary Cray, Swanley, Otford, Kemsing, Borough Green & Wrotham,
West Malling, East Malling, Barming, Maidstone East

23 February 85
The conning-tower surfaces into
"An age of information uncertainty"
And simultaneously "built into those systems
Are processes of innovation & change"
Inhabit a maze of vectors. Interference.
Pac-man reels in Ariadne's thread

27 February 85
No such thing as repetition
Because when a thing happens for the first time
It has not already happened
And when it happens again it has happened before
So inevitably at once there is a difference
And the difference is caused by memory

9 March 85
Cat on a slate roof stalks
Finds an opening, pigeons cluster
It is the sense that anything could happen
The sense of potential – weather changes
Rapidly a cold front approaching
From the Atlantic

17 March 85
12.05 am: After a dry frosty night with patches of freezing fog
It will be dry & quite sunny, but Northern Ireland
Will have outbreaks of sleet or snow

18 March 85
8.50 am: Mail arrives, blue dot security marks
Embellishing, evidence of the network
9.55 pm: The social sphere encircled by a drum's rim
Men press coins & banknotes on a blind singer's forehead

20 March 85
4.45 pm: Catfood, bread, brandy, typewriter repair
7–11 pm: Saxophone solo & ensemble, circular breathing

21 March 85
7.55 am: Radio resonates in bone & musculature
Coffee machine hiccoughs, vapour trails
Discharged by skin contact
12 noon: Power station
12.02 pm: "Pound touching $1.1745, chancellor keeps drop to ½%
& nods in 14% mortgages."
11.07 pm: Bach, Sonata in C major for solo violin, BWV 1005
"The cognitive & the affective are reunited."

31 March 85
(Summer time begins)
9.05 pm: Helicopters in formation
10.05 pm: "Assume that it constantly changes, but that you do not notice the change."
11.59 pm: (entry blank)

October 1985:
Leigh-on-Sea, the up platform

Pied wagtails were twitching on a flat field, maybe football pitch
Before the brightness faded in the estuary& gantries darkened
        to a Sunday flush
Attention the 42 up 2 bells a red light lights
                        but
42 never came, 88 walks by on the platform carrying a tote bag
        total silence & 2 videos to watch
And on the other side is just a deserted car-park at the heart
        of the horizon
Two lovers entwining their speech is the shadow of that silence

Clover on the permanent way gathers amber light to itself,
        engines begin to make reverberate the lunar estuary
Night settles on corroded tanks & desolate rubble worked loose
        from the planet, white cars with white fish smell the
        scales fired into wallpaper sky
                        and
Polished steel sings a warning to the imperial sweet lives of
        young benched posers hoping to get clear this month

Lyrical Ballets

1990

for Wendy Mulford

Ars Poetica

Pointing to the words
with the words only
makes your hand ache
your head still in fog.

If previewing a comedian
the first thing you wouldn't ask
is what jokes would he tell.
And similarly the road to there

starts from here always; no map
scans correctly at long intervals;
tambourines weigh against the
body's asserted pleasure

points, just audible, as if
they were chemical components.
Law regulates the respiration
of the body but poetry

unscrambles that again
the repeated mind pitch lucidity
as foreign to hypnosis as to analysis
of what's to become.

I Want a Sort of Lingering

I want a sort of lingering
effect a negligible margin

not sticky not hallucination like
an optical clump that trickles

But where there's time to breathe
and a brilliant gesture like a kiss

Dream

1

I was locked in a dream
inside knowledge deserted
diesel locomotive
in Africa, perhaps fruit-eating.
An erogenous zone, molecular
not fossil evidence, saying I know
how to walk, & these bones
are part of my body.
Hip bones & thigh bones,
neck/head articulation. Immediately
I was on the airplane,
you could see the white lining, someone
kept complaining about it, I woke

2

as a seagull
shook itself in full flight across
where snow was falling, & blowing
powdery off an opposite roof
and you were on the other side of a city
looking into the interior
falling
short of completion. No longer
named, I'd entered absurdity & you
were a match flare away
in this tiniest world an ontology
perched in the thick of it.

Breakfast in Bermondsey

The ubiquitous hue, a stream
that led through from deep heat,
appeared even as the phased roar
dipped. Nel mezzo, etc.
The 2 specks resolved themselves
onto the middle arm, slopes the
valley. Hallucinations of breakfast,
quite unlike the normal nondescript
brown of the "thing itself",
so soft that they only registered
lightly golden, illuminating the passage,
widened into sharply defined milky areas
that hugged my own perceptions.
Faint freckles assembled on a white
shirt, observed at new resolutions.

Begging Comparison

There are things in a person's life which cannot be
accounted for.

And upon that cardinal, all else hinges.

We stress positive connotation.

As soon as we have what we want, all others are
returned with a "try us again" tag.

We wake at 6, dreaming of toilets. The pain is better,
but.

We sit down at the piano and start to shake.

Are we to lurk in the shrubs for an illicit
illumination?

What heavy sky will our morning selves be in the
thick of?

Rosebay Willowherb
(after Antonio Machado)

I went to the house you once lived in
It was the only sunny day of the summer

There was borage and mint
On the sill, burst through urban decay

Long flowered, the years have spent since
Perhaps there is no more such language

Please Use This Side of the Door

They make a lovely couple
a pint of best & a white lady
slopping back till she radiates
and his learning curve vaults the starry hosts.

Outside and
all at once the main drag
fingers his coat, oh I didn't know
you could dance, she remarks,
there's hidden
depths to me, he says, & steps
out onto the golden tarmac
not looking.

3D Spectacles of the Heart

I am split in 2 when I look at you

One half of me thinks love
and sees the normal money
right there on the screen
golden slumbers
heated by a mysterious internal source

The other half thinks love
and overwhelms
to precipitate what is
out of what might be

You are & are not in the story but whatever
I'm out of the damn tunnel now.

Report from the Community Park Committee

This is simple—
the park is for
ANYBODY
to enjoy, as long
as
all aspects
are interim

Winter isn't
used to the full
the wooden fences & the shrubs
are beginning to grow
we're deciding on essential equipment
we're also finding some teeth
& these are being sorted out.

A Lyric Poem in the Era of High Capitalism

The world is: new vistas
The world is: your oyster
The world is: crashing about your EARS

Please maintain this ironic detachment

the light fantastic
lyric
assimilating everything in sight

The Big Heat Remake

At a very obvious transactional level
Money for discourse
It could've been really terrific & authentic
But then a stupid thing happens
You're not allowed to work or not work
Tant pis
This is a form of relation like any other
A woman removes the shadow from the shadow

Homage to Catatonia

This is one of my most
Favourite pieces it's very lifelike
His mind oscillates passionately

It was there to discover
But not to prove
Observer & observed built right into it

Close enough to get
To the very heart of the pigment
Spirals of the vortex

When they stop existing they become
Lovely soil & grass & other solid things
It got too hot & I came out

I grasped knowledge
And there was no other way out
In the thermal an incident out of time

I remember leaving
Getting my scarf then
Nothing

Another floor slewed sideways
It wasn't the dreams it was
What happened after

Lineaments

Today
I eliminated part of the mountain
and it's only because
I did not think of you once
till now the early evening starlings
at it, luminosity fills the stems
I doze off & the glass darkens
something enters by the door I cannot
yet make out its lineaments

Speak to me
our voices skip the wire /
are interfered with
a soft mistake that lights us up

like the sun did as we walked
not by the river in the city
among terrific machines

An Exchange, or a Transition

The thread of it, lucid
stills mine, the day begins
almost simultaneously

A word to denote the unplanned
sunny slow spacious & friendly
our work below gulls

Stretch & flap
the megamix downstairs she
"cried buckets" to the echo

A bright enduring love
but it feels like a door
but no, there are no doors

Glass shines in the spring
its colour is indeterminate
the strangest thing

Under Construction

Lemony taste. It has no liveliness, any
shape; you have the criteria bang to
rights there. He works into the night,
singing *rainfall keeps dropping on my*
head. The bowl's cracked, the plant
bruised, scenting the air conditioning
the fabric a gap in building buckled.
Stain on the tap's here to stay.
Whether bowels shift or no, you can get
the rest of the room to resonate with
the architrave and skirting board, a
bare bulb off-centre displacing clarity
from the twice-covered corner. Linger
awhile; skip her hoot. Down the road,
breadfruit, plantains, collapsed ginger;
into the packet rubble a sink dives
uncannily; the reception is off. As
when balm flourishes from damaged root
stock; piles briskly skeletal mud
returns strata to commerce, so flight
finds its extension returned in a
parabolic radio window. Sleep cloaks
his hands; tongue cleaves to the groove.

Song from the Japanese

Tin has been suspended
So has aluminium stock
Pushing out the elementals
Down at the bedrock

Commodities dazzle patient crowds
Till they virtually disappear
If I had my way I'd build myself
An office block right here

And dance & dance in it
The whole day long
With my neon love from the hot baths
Singing this song

Rosa's Pictures

This is squares
This is steps
This is also steps
This is Ken
This is stripes
This is all of us

Good Science

1992

Preface:
A note to the reader on the use of this book and possible responses

See clearly with clear eyes. Be strong, harmonic and geological. Shun high-tech special effects. As a constant reminder of the possibilities, hold up a kaleidoscope to "our expanding universe". Do not always trust machines. Demonstrate a dispersal pattern reminiscent of, or at least seeming to be a synthesis. In the service of compassion, reduce all human aspirations to the brute matter of existence. Look at the world unflinchingly in the grey morning light. "Create a system, or be enslaved by another's." Relevant systems appear simultaneously as unsolved mystery and as ample evidence. Demonstrate relevance. Relevant systems have no content (specific) but plenty of formal designations (variable). Demonstrate variation. They spread, and cause the perspective to tilt; but they have no intent. Demonstrate intent. Where there is no intent, there is no dance, where there is no dance, there is no exactness, where there is no exactness, there is no death. Open the telephone book at random, call the number, when the person answers give the person the news, and hang up. Do not attempt explanation. Do not apologise.

Contort; invest a song. Practise "the fruity O, the piquant short i"; use "occasionally sarcastic typography". Call it the language. Hint at a place beyond language. Alternately speak, and indicate the silence beyond speech. Alternately add meaning to events, and take away their meaning. Do improvisation to pay the rent. Speak several languages; reject all language. Think in your mouth. Believe in verbal magic. Go on speech strike for six months. Remember "the code is not adequate to what needs to be said; it is not the language". Create something modern and intrinsic, sensitive and strong. Treat words with the contempt they deserve.

Learn everything you can, and forget everything you have learnt; do this on alternate days. Look at yourself straight in the face. Scorn the blandishments of songbirds. Laugh uncontrollably. Waste time. Groan. Throb. Consider whether "art is crime". Go to jail anyway. Stifle. Steam. Congest. Melt. Extinguish. Pour. Staunch. Curse. Sleep. Put the question squarely. Escape. Forget everything. Panic. Take measures to illustrate your disquiet. Come to your senses. Don't be so stupid. Destroy the cadence of the line, the beauty of the image, the aptness of the metaphor. Cultivate a deliberately lush and sensuous vocabulary, and then prune it savagely. Better still, shun all metaphors. Cultivate misunderstanding. Be reasonable. Collect useful facts, and facts about facts. Make them into a structure that is completely useless. Collect useless facts, and make them into a useful structure. Make textures and structures in the tentative region of the untried. Make a bridge for scholars, then at a crucial moment blow up the bridge. Set fire to all manuscripts. Make "every sentence ... a critique of reason". Persist. Involve everybody. Implicate everybody. Ingest. Undermine homoeostasis in language with a sense of balance overtipped by the non-programmed, i.e. anything could happen. Remember sensation of form is sensation of flow.

Replace experience with language. Replace form with design. Open all windows. Lie on the carpet. Think carefully. Abolish the floor. Eat your words. Destroy information. Nuzzle cups, bathe archipelagos, suck gold, number gravel, lift silk, carry animals, manufacture grief, parse hallucinations, swallow embers, suspect hostages, supervise deserts, ridicule buildings, hurl bones, research hunger, simmer books, sniff electricity, crush parapets, imagine clothes.

Never discount the opacity of language. Never attempt to communicate. Never form a kind of shell or armour round the subject. Never make absolute sense. By no means shun exactness. Do not attempt to make sense of "our culture". Never write what you expect to have written. Do not concern yourself with lyric significance. "Use the telephone instead of writing the poem." Avoid floral-phallic imagery. Do not however forget pleasure in the erotic multiplicity of sense. Never compromise. Never close for lunch. Reject validation. Accept over-determination.

Be marginal and heat-seeking. Be glittering, leggy, inevitable. Be agitational, molecular, powerful, disparate, innumerable, blank, necessary, accurate, conscious, communal, conservative. Encourage relentless hope. Hope for "a liberty of unimaginable opulence". Hope for "a purely linguistic world". Hope for "a kind of chemical solution". Hope for "a state in which speech is at the same time more primitive and more sophisticated than in ordinary usage". Hope for "the transformation of the vertical". Surprise yourself. Astonish others. Uncover "a content that pushes against social taboos otherwise not only untransgressed but unknown". Hope for "a textual body recognised by the fact that it is always endless, without ending". Take scientific notes. "Gulp down the tawny herds." Hope for "an explosion of verbal glass". Differentiate. Invent the language everybody already speaks. Make a contract with language; then break the contract. Imitate everybody; originate nothing. Tell lies rather than tell half-truths. Live without memory. Surround yourself with resources, and wait. Get rid of all resources, and act now.

Thanks to: Guillaume Apollinaire, William Blake, Lyn Hejinian, Hélène Cixous, Paul Goodman, John Vernon, Frank O'Hara, Jeff Nuttall, Arthur Rimbaud, Nikola Vaptsarov

GOOD SCIENCE

Good Science

The drill sergeants break up the only road we've got
The angry woman rings it starts to rain
I state my case on the basis of need
You shoot it down on the basis of want

This week has given me a new grasp of particle physics
You see how the glands in your throat do swell
So profitability extends to the Silurian layers
The Dow is up the unit starts to break down

A light plane trails red fly north-west orient
I've managed to lie down on the floor just once
The embarrassment factor peaked now & again
Neoclassicism was a reaction to this "dangerous future"

My legs started to shake uncontrollably
They are not objects but networks of relationships
She was smoking & talking for the first time
A threequarter century rhythm punctuates diurnal priorities

Morosely a pearly king & queen get off the train
A gunshot spoils the tidal rhythm
Take away the underlying phrase-length & improvisation remains
Does fortune play the strumpet with me now?

It was a projection outward of active perception
It was my muscles starting to open up
Maybe get sunflowers for the sunny wall
Her voice is a beautiful city that doesn't exist

We spent a most pleasant evening thank you
Liberated from the bar-line the grid-lit slabs reverberate
I tend to dissolve into the usual
You couldn't take more than an hour so left

After a heavy day the book was no more than adequately clear
The pound started trembly the board sent the dollar down
Now there's no objective way of measuring space
So the room moves into & out of phase with my conception

The elephant house is blinded with plywood
It contains the ghosts that language doesn't need
I could have gone to the music but didn't feel like it
You could have had salt beef rice & mixed pickle

Small children lay multicoloured hoops on the new tarmac
Contrast the yellow-grey gloom & the white glare
Extended intervals are occurring
It pervades my whole life at the moment

I bought a book on the subject & immediately felt guilty
They stayed in bed arbitrarily distanced
The big building is full of really crazy people
The man is 22 & has 2 tattoos

She cites brachiation as the original divergence
Scored for 6 bass clarinets & 6 contrabass clarinets
You dovetail neatly into the above stuff
I wake up I open the refrigerator I don't know where I am

A Walk by the Vanished Powdermill

a sonata for w.m.

1

Which begins: an early morning
in a high European capital.
The band marches past half-
disassembled scaffolding
hits orange vertigo somewhere
between the majestic sweep
of the Andes & bad plumbing.

Trombones &
notes in shallow baskets
& much later about 12 poets
drunk below a viaduct —

Into this mess swoops a siren a monument
a savings bank the moment
démenagement slips your lips a stranded
tourist crocodile gapes the gap extends
to half tended gardens scooped
a disappeared gunpowder magazine
overlooking the confluence.
This powerful wall is almost breathtaking
we go to the very nice "Pétrusse" park
down freedom street
we enjoy viewing the viaduct
a redoubtable redoubt is manifest here.

Also the museum is closed
fermé, fermato, cerrado.

2

A three-way babble
in variegated light
white blue red
that's OK so street level
you can see anything
that way never begin
again never return lost light
pressure at the base of the neck
in flooded colour
dream or drift down a sky slope
lose the city

continually

dissolve or drown in your body
hold your voice

the book slips from your hand this
fragile admission's very lovely/terrifying
mingled with perfume & heavy
shivery changeable day.
Oh wake up for heaven's sake
kick out the loops.
There are certain crucial elements missing
in this room but love is in it.

3

Where has the powdermill disappeared to?
It's not there on the magnificent hilltop.

Nor down below in the mysterious valley
where you're not supposed to go.

Regard the bridge. It weighs thus many
metric tonnes I forget. There are 119

others plus of course the viaduct which presides
over our ramshackle funny lives.

4

I'm sitting in the civic square now waiting
for you to come by. On the stand
the band plays A Life on the Ocean Wave
the burgers strut the tables are jolly
red & white the cloths nipped to them by
steel callipers. Your absence is manifest everywhere.
Long cables hold the trees together
they are like cables of love
but here is an interruption.

One of those where you don't can't
get it all but it makes your brain

stand on end with its implications how
long can this go on? We have the rest
of our lives for such grand passion & lack
of co-ordination and it didn't matter
then energy flooded back:
do you have the picture? with the paper
held up front? what pattern will emerge?

As it happens this wonderful
flavour explodes in your mouth
like *il pubblico della poesia*
applauding without as one or
tossing sawdusty bread rolls
into this hotel room perchance
which is a kind of non-euclidean
space which is sweet —

Cross it out.

Put sugar in your coffee.
Kick up the blanket. Utterly
change your life.

Luxembourg, spring 1987

Blaze

for Joseph Beuys

Semen and
menstrual blood
stain the shelf
surround

an inventor
of metaphors
an idiot
refuses

wholly
a tool without
blood on it
means naked

people with
animals took
him out of this
crash heap

so he
related such
material to
the social body

to a screen
image to a
broken line
suddenly

crumbled it
looked
secure but
blood reaches

to the throat
the terror
region
a drum rally

into a steeple
geese fly
the basic
stuff of risk

luminous
through the
webbed skeleton
or through

assembled dirt
for contemplation
a small book
during the war

immediately
possible for
human discipline
meaning

more basic
to warmth
more basic to
coldness

collapse began
to damage
the rule
structure

to come
to that again
wailing through
the long

work
in wood stain
his courage
phases

in fields
far from holy
flocks or
trails

coarse gritty
abandoned
moist poignant
a kind of

real other
excavation
of nail-paring
shadow

lasts for
1,000 years
then vacates
the building

physical flesh
to become
windstream
a new sculpture

a wound that
doesn't
know its own
price

a gauge
of what is
likely
to take place

a crown that's
melted to an
animal born
gold

mixed with
alcohol
transformed
to peace

or a tree
with a
stone is
beautiful

Lashed to the Mast

1

The timer clicks
the flame bursts
the children
were found wandering in the
garden
— afraid
to spin madly
into this white book —
"the walls just fell away"
"I had expected
serious injuries even
some fatalities so I was
pleasantly surprised"
watch the nets a
crisis in the nasal passages
they will decide
whether to
testify
you know that
heaven &
earth was
lashed
"I did not paint it
to be enjoyed"

*

Blood
enters the painting & a
weary languor fills my wallet

while up
stairs the sirocco burns
the leaves off the pods off

oh my
          when will the summers of old
          return to transfigure the future

being
          a representation of what you can
          never have like California sex

so that
          we shall meet again in the fields but
          shan't remember our names or why

and call
          mother mother it's no use the water's
          burning the wind the water the sun

*

One evening the sky looks
like a Rothko heavy pink-grey
bearing down on a band of ice-blue
the next it's a mottled burst
spread from its milky heart behind
the offices it is driving you quite mental
yet hopeful but strange
lumpish cloud returns today
to hide the rest of the universe

*

Worries about Money
     make chemical changes
          in the mind which are boring
in the blood
          stains fade into the post-

modern pattern
of the bed
which could be runic
all the sixes
clickety click
the station
meets the train
with a shy
smile
halfway
goddess in high
heels
(white) (representing
Money)
welcomes travellers to our
Heritage
economic growth &
prospects of artistic wonder
pointed the phone at the Moon
said we'll shoot it down
a planet hovers
perilously

*

It is a terrible thing
to be walking on a string
and never
to fall

I did this all night long
and I was not wrong
to wake

it was not morning nor bloody

my new home
’s roof is patched
its downpipes coming away
but I wake
in it

it is in my veins & heart
beating & making a weak
form like a sentence implied
by its punctuation

or like four walls imply
a space

*

Oh
such
wonderful
style
posing
all over
the
super-
structure
in your
designer
jeans
& being
consumed
with the
in-
effable —
bought of
ponderables —
though all thought
fled
from your head

six shamans
          or men or she-men
     invade your dream
               my bloody Valentine

*

At the end
all that will
be left is
the depth of
sunlight fall-
ing on the
ancient trucks
way beyond
your capacity
to comprehend
and the sense
of a name
that constantly
eludes your lips
and leads you
into delusion
that language
is merely
a question
of naming

2

Two people speak &
a third observes
from afar
their body gestures their eyebrows

& from this
draws a conclusion

A fourth says the
terrible words

And a fifth & sixth —

Can they tell you a secret
he was in Mexico with a friend
the building buckles
into the gulf which
forms in the interstices
of our syntax

And a train roars past
carrying the seventh

to the point of no return

*

As a star turns blue
in gathering crépuscule

you become that small pleasure

just drop your shoulders
and the word skips out

it's only a word

But a word is worth
a thousand pictures

I thought I saw a kestrel
fly over the high street

moving its darkness swiftly
below the pearly light

the clouds made

*

I do not spurn
the hand of friendship
and yet
there is so little
that I can say

when the red jewels
pass into the night
I am so hot
I shiver with it
hands on the bricks

there was a road
we began

and it is not ended

sometimes there are fire-
works
beyond the gilded
buildings

I think of you then
& all the selves
you could have been

*

    Strange
        thought: to
continue
        undecidably so
    for
        where events
    have seemed to
        crash
            &
                billow
    they have fallen
        kindly
            in the end

    & it is no part
        of face
            value
to deny them
        their momentum
    of speculative
        grace

*

There was never enough wine
        poetry's line has been cut
a berk lays claim to its energy
        yet kinship is fostered even
across the ocean of dreams
        in a celebrated scrawl
sweet burned chicken
        secure against wind & money
fills three ravening stomachs
        she mends her broken house
while he prepares to leave his
        & both part from the third
where the foundations rise

& plane trees lie akin
to a slew of happiness

*

A
quite
appalling
hamburger
marks
our parting
anew
(whoever
someone
thought we were)
across
the ocean
of foolishness
a raft
we
have
named
wisdom

3

Quilted by what sea
my blunt fingers
snuggle up
to a world of wonders
customs/pigeons/
Bantu warriors/laundrette/
abandoned supermarket
salty through the throat

headlights flicker
            on the dark bodies
in the theatre
            with no name

*

(from the Spanish)

As soon as I fall asleep
there are the spaces
where my face becomes snow
high, in the territory

And when I embark
with my heart in shadow
I take this writing with me
below the level of consequence

And each night is a new
infancy, of a profile
sufficient to destroy
the language of my rusty years

*

(for Olivier Messiaen)

A Paradise of
Birds
Tropicals the
Night

When the music
Stops

It is as though
Nothing
Begins

*

Just a bright desk-lamp
& the warm
cuddle of the
air between
these 4 walls takes you through
to the mid-
point of the day
when you repair
to the Star across the road
for sustenance
in a foggy
dream of a
space between the fragilities

*

Dig into
the
depths a

wish
wells
up

(is it
choreography or is it
dance?)

it's on the
cards

it's in the
stars

blind we
bat
a lid
in the
black
night

a
brilliance
beyond

*

Sluttish prevarication &
dreadful sloth
creep upon me in the sadness
of winter
my friend of strange
foggy furloughs

My sunny days
are spangled upon the folds
of memory flashing up
in fits I love to behold
it is at such times I'd saddle
a recalcitrant mule & take to the lemon
groves that braid some mountain

where the Catholic monarchs
confront the Moorish dynasties
across a word-processed valley
or across the orbit of a TV satellite
in the dying of the sun

But the white noise
of a no-signal screen remains –
were I to reach to switch
that off
I'd switch the darkness on

July–December 1988

DEEP SONG

Granada / El Chorro / Ronda, 1987

Deep Song

May a small thing become large
& make of such worry a tired fabric
that seems delicate? In the kitchen,
white food. Smoke fades
linearly. Dogs peter into the distance
a roule of disturbance in the night's suburb
in the night's night, covering half
a still discovered globe. The roofs
bunch. What can't be said is
how deep it goes, into the dark,
a plaint, or a cycle of intention—
a left hanky on a golden lit table
a couple of books offering content
its substitute, the small medicine
anticipating its disease. But those hills
wasting into mist, where are they?
the lace upon them & the colour
blue? Before them stand the buildings of a kingdom
half integrated with the wood
& offering the dead sun its reflectance
a facade & colonnade for the entry
of the weapons of nostalgia that
stupid cry of the heart
representing trophies, though
presently far & immune
from such shapely rhetoric wanting
out of love's habit to hold a life & sensing
uncertainty. Colour fails through
three inclined trapezoidal panels
& stars of eight & sixteen points
decorate the whole composition. A lovely
geometric surrounds its most solemn acts
& beyond, the towers become water

& just fade away. Water does
converge. And that makes a cue
an infinitely reversible sign
for return to night, the city, all that this
means. That is to say this
species of absence out of which
& towards which every page spirals
so making of presence & absence
the coordinates. And in the cunningly
divided room with rectangular areas in shadow
you will also believe this. Or better,
you will abandon belief & cover
the fretted self arrayed
with text & fragrant hibiscus
flowers in another night, in a night
that is not this already slipping from you.

A Generating Station in Andalucía

    Green — I want you —
Not the mysterious reservoir —
        Nor its appearance in a hot valley
    As a still element, perhaps of grief — no —
        Green of the north
How novel it looks
    on the ground & on the trees

    I want to wake up
        In my new home — in the city
Green, rhythmic
        traffic of it steals sleep
    From the gathering autumn

Breathe deep & simultaneously
        The stars hide their turbulence

Behind a pall that inserts
Above the still dark air a thought

Is the self of thought
the same as the self
that writes the thought?
the command centre at the
heart of a mountain?
Is it
the difference between
ritual & habit? The dark
hills wait. The sky
is black. Where
did a thought come
from? & what faint
sound from the lit bars
at night will take me
back there?

The shining flat
water reflects four
terrible floodlights
among derricks &
piers. Beyond the dark
hills are the black
mountains & beyond,
the unimagined sky. Four
lights hum in night's
fragrance. The Pleiades
above the mountain
blur.

And now that green is flecked
It whites up on you

What do I care
as you dive into the pool

The water is not separate
From the body, and the body
As it moves through the water
Is not wet

Only as you move into the sun does the water cling
And become separate

Far below, and scarcely
perceived — lemon
or olive groves braided
across a mountain, scarcely
do snake track, light
pools, dust shading
to deep green in bluish
air, cling to the surfaces.

You go up that mountain & immediately
you go to sleep
It washes your mind
Out from the inside –
You are discovered by a gypsy —

You sit outside on the terrace typing
And the mountains – more blue now –
& their braids –
I was talking to you about my friend:
We were on a high road amid white
flowers & eucalyptus, it was only
when I woke I knew

But it was real, or it partook of something
You wouldn't even call real, you're
in it, actually

You go to sleep, & it washes
your mind out –
I go to the mountain & there is a little tank
Of still green water I look into —
It's hot, & the silence
Bounces thus off the hills around
I take a photograph of the mountain

Up the valley advanced
Tariq's army covered by
earth. Now bones, store-
houses, entry places
& wells appear. A
thousand years arch
out of the rock, a cock
crow greets short
rain spotting the tiles
in grey. The sun begins
to push its whiteness
through, but cover slips
up from the horizon.

Look at me
I don't know you now
You move through the water
Afraid to touch its limitless
limits –

We were both sitting on the edge
    Of the stagnant water tank he said
"So long" & dropped
    It was some years before he hit the water –

Your keys & espadrilles
    Laid neatly on a stone beside you

Half a porcelain cup
on the terrace's round
table's circled by a fly.
The breeze begins.

I found you lying
as though asleep
on the side of a
mountain, as though
you'd got off the train
of thought & failed
to get back on.

Look at me, he said – the water
    Sparkling in the sun because it moves

You sit on the terrace in your dark
    Glasses & your headscarf in the photograph
        That was before –

Old buzzing
fly languidly
persists, nearby —

heaves blackish
body in erratic
motion from
corner to corner
of the almost
darkened room —

And now the thought has gone, and
only its words remain —
Their demands blur
into the wash
Green.
I want —

Rilke Driving School

Composing a latter-
Day *ghazal* here
Am I leaning
On the corner
Of the *Calle*
Carlos Marx, a
Taste as of
Lemon in my
Mouth, a real
Nexus of energy!
While Rilke,
Now transformed, a
Metal man
Stands in the
Garden of the
Hotel Queen
Victoria, Ronda,
Gazes into a
Future that

Hangs perilously
Limpid over the
Chasm, a fever
That becomes
Almost palpable. What
Substance wavers
And weaves? Who
Do you cling
To when it
Happens? when the
World opens up
Under your feet,
When its substance
Vanishes, what is
Your resource when
No meaning
Happens, when
Stuff is rent?
And why
Do I recall
This on the
Train much
Later, gold giving
Way to silver
In the cloud
Streaks that
Halo industrial
Estates & playing
Fields of south
London? But I
See it's the
Wrong train, the
Network must be
Negotiated anew.
I love you
Very much, even
After you reach
A certain point
On your progress

Down the hill,
When the sun
Disappears behind
Some crystals &
Suddenly you are
In shadow. Not
Too dismal, chucking
Out tons of
Rubbish, I'm re-
Born, almost.
Perhaps momentous
Changes have left
Me physically.

*

Rilke: I am
Older & sometimes
Physically horizontal.
Here is the
Photo, little
Poet with his
Hand resting on
Big poet. Hmm.
His bag &
Camera thus.
Oh to be
Metal, to no
Longer crumble
Fast from the
Pressure but to
Rust slowly
Under a deep
Blue Spanish sky,
To be metal
And glass. Why
Cling? It's no
Use when momentous
Changes impend.

For example, this
Evening a car
Whisks me off
To a surreal
Interview, I just
Had to sit
Back in the
Sticky leatherette.
I love you,
I was seized
With a desperate
Fear I dared
Not convey,
Trembling in the
Bedroom much later.
Roots crack, seeds
Germinate, two
Locomotives fall in
Love down a
Suburban chasm. The
Fear has dissipated
Like foam
Upon the water.
You approach me:
Temperatures do
Now fluctuate.

*

Yesterday I was
All arms &
Thumbs, nervously
Circling the flat.
And a wintry
Light all week.
Today I am
Walking on air,
I am almost
Above the brink

Of the gorge
In that garden
With Rilke to
Blot my idiot
Remarks into
Its waters. We
Walk calmly,
Discussing, it is
Almost as though
We're in the
World. *Cut.*
Put on my
Scarf & walk
Into the winter-
Less winter
Whose first few
Moments baffle my
Brain, playing Muslim
Blues; a demon
Closed my eyes
In the garden
Of the Queen
Victoria, your right
Thigh against me.
But you were
Never there; I
Love you, it's
An emergency.
Buildings shudder
To their deaths
But your grip
Is firm. Someone
Is breathing
Slowly on the
Train while a
Walkman idly
Spits. The train
Comes to a
Shuddering halt,

Awakes me from
Dream. Hesitation.
Glad of these
Contours, my hands
Change colour in
Celebration of you.
Sunshine is
In the picture
To which we
Shall certainly
Return. A poem
Is like a
Story, except liquid
With echo. White
Letters far below
Indicate the unassailable
Distance to square
Fields, the colours
Oily the timber
Stacked the estate
Real the plunder
Partly the water
Flat with reedy
Clog & animal
Magic, lemons
Left to rot
In the warm
Heart of the
Old country. A
Poem is like
A story except
Nobody knows
What it means.
Woke up before
It was light,
Eager to
Let the day
Begin. In my
Fitful dream

There was even
More happy
Confusion. I go
Up that mountain
And return, legs
Trembling, speaking
Nonsense through an
Empty tube that
Boggles the
Archives, the shadow
Moving on the
Wall, the landscapes
Beneath us, &
Roads of especial
Touristic interest, i.e.
Terrifying. Dance
Of light in
Water. The glitter-
Ing fragments
Wept. It was
Because I never
Thought there was
Anyone who
Could tell me
What they
Were. You are
Magnified a million
Times. Water moves
In your eyes
Briefly. White
Light on tennis
Courts, on bowling
Green, the ropes
Of steel.

BAD SIRENS

After a Season the Syntax Falls

for Doug Oliver

Through your half-window
    a little blues must fall
    on midnight's alien heart
    morale fragments

And you don't want the visit
    to end, the terrible new
    that hugger-mugger steals the echo
    while knowing its origin fled

But it wasn't choice, & weakness
    fills your body, giving
    it colour & stain & every
    rhetoric of the interval

The evening was white at first but
    blackening to ripeness
    the language stayed on hold
    the roofs portended

A perfume of turbid
    rain, a great plain oak
    laid on its side among bracelets
    among the streets

A rusty tip, a wisp of blue
    solicited your viral ecstasies
    entered the audit like a ghost
    a white band of dust around your brains

When from no time a bad siren screamed
    into the night — the white

narcissus must grow loaded now
your hand on the cup dishevels

You wake into a swoon
a barium meal lights up your heart
in the temperate city
you will never see again

You're in the street: a crowd
outside the surgical building
waits to be threaded, three
by three up the crooked wood

To a fortress, a dark fact
a horseshoe steeply raked
above the bare brilliance where it's
crammed, condemned to watch

Where young attendants
come & go, chalk scribbles
on the conference board, then more
till the composition obscures

They feed white noise in
to make believe it's quiet
a woman says: "It's a small world
either that or a big hospital"

What is this place? a surplus value
of meaning? the way a shadow
falls, drains into poetry, the way
a shadow falls the way a shadow falls

An elephant bears a turret, frankly
naff, a flare illuminates the place
of silence, engine blanketed
cloud-cover building grid

A bank of 20 screens
& a glaze of money on each one

you feel that it all must have
happened a long time ago

The numbers rise & fall
implacably serene you place
a child's compass next the cathode ray
its needle spins round madly

How briefly this machine
flickers under glass & then
is still — sleeves your flesh
into the vinyl

What was a factory or church
becomes a theme park
what was a hospital becomes
a hologram of commerce

Its first replica, your father
trembles on the bed
your mother has no verbs
for her mistake

Places the logical value "false"
within a cell, the heart
which generates an error
a principle of depth

It's unredeemable, a botch
turns mental sex into a monster
to be done in comprehensively
in the place of silence

Where the residual heat is found
to crack walls, no ventilation
no light, an inside job
classed as a family

Where a man with a spike
hacks at a piece of composite

a venerable shibboleth
an assessment of trauma

Where a sad pale one approaches
on the uneven platform
as a voice begins again to chide
endlessly: Mind the gap

Who extends a supplicant hand
needing to go to a coastal town
needing for this six pounds
you give him one

Or at another station one approaches
matching sadness with belief
needing to go to the Horn of Africa
needing your answer to his question

On the actual train, a lovely
couple: he holds a giant tin
of coffee, rusting all the while
she cuddles a restless guinea-pig

Another leans against a jamb
he cannot move he can
not move, save to launch a sluggish
Indian meal on the wine-dark tarmac

All go to the enterprise meltdown
though the glass be smashed
and the wafer skin grey
that held Communitas

Serrated, almost noble once
though the very veins broke
in a welter of logic bombs
where the oaks do lie

There are no maps here but
a hoarding sells you worms

with designer-brain finance
the public flock to null

Thwarted by thrones
so evidently respectful
not anchored in sufficiency
but tethered in want

Fitting to be savaged
& thrust into a neuro-surge
which is really a market that
masquerades as body scan

Like a pricing-gun, tension
speaks, stops, stutters
the heat abates & turns to thin rain
outside the place of silence

You stumble to the street —
in its broken booth a phone rings
endlessly all-night TV reflected in a window
victims & supermarket trolleys

A woman ghost — "I've been here 20 years
waiting for a 188" — & socialism's born
& dies, while unctuously a distant radio
grieves your mouth explodes

In a vast pool of undrained mud
parked hatchbacks left, first sound
of birdsong, a rusty tip a wisp
of blue, & mad poetry fills your sense

All this you see through
your high lustre window
or is it your punch blushed
face that rebounds?

Are they the same old bones that
rattle in the same old tin?

does half of the imagery
curve into the same error?

You are there in heat the
colour closing down
down 40, rose falling
glad of a transient

Through your half-window
a little blues must fall
a scent of history trembling
at the wrists of never

Lexical Dub

"Secret secret never seen
secret secret ever green"
– popular song

Police glossolalia haunt radio heavy wind
Instruments of use in time of war
From here to Texas burgeoning

An offence an offence (as officially defined)

We wage war on all the animals that come to live with us

An offence such an offence

Teams finger the ethics of punishment
A gunboat to Morocco had become an epidemic The Agadir
On blood red screen man washes car with hosepipe crisis, 1911
That person shall be guilty of a misdemeanour
Approaches or is in the neighbourhood of or enters
Each occupied square is surrounded by 8 squares
Any prohibited place possession or control
Looks like colour xerox & feels like a total effect

Any sketch plan model article note document
Or information like when real blood appears
On video screen music
Swells to gothic cancerous zombies superimpose
If any person communicates or retains he
Shall be liable to imprisonment with or without
Hard labour
Any work of defence arsenal factory
Dockyard camp ship telegraph or signal station or office
Any ship arms or other materials or instruments
Of use in time of war or any plans or documents
Demand paralysis respect for rule of law
Any railway road way or channel
Declared by a Secretary of State to be a prohibited place
Shall be a prohibited place

*

Edition of *The London Programme* on heroin addiction, transmitted 13.iv.84, London Weekend TV

Starts with £5 scag bags on the council estates
Or any place used for gas water or electricity works
Ends with novocaine mainlined into tongues
To protect official secrets & get us out
Of a bad situation vis-a-vis that which endures
Or any place where any ship arms or other materials
Or instruments of use in time of war

*

Speech by Lord Haldane, 1911; see article by Peter Kellner in *New Statesman*, 6.iv.84

Not many months ago we found in the middle of the
Fortifications at Dover an intelligent stranger
Who explained his presence by saying
He was there to hear the singing of the birds
Any offence an offence the offence the offence
Incites or counsels or attempts to procure

An offence an offence an offence that offence

Two men got up to speak but both were forcibly pulled down
By their neighbours after they had uttered

Such an offence an offence such an offence

A few sentences again they were pulled down
By their neighbours the vote 107–10 (500 abstentions)
One hot Friday afternoon in August
If a justice of the peace is satisfied
Things went a bit far he may grant a search warrant
Authorising any constable to seize
If necessary by force and to search and to search
Any sketch plan model article note or document
All acts which are offences when committed or when committed
Having been or being about to be committed

Official Secrets Act, enacted 22.viii.11, after going through all stages in the Commons in less than an hour

*

In 1981 crucial
Molotov cocktails make white goods blush
Crunched underfoot in a skin of acid rain
From here to Texas looks like colour xerox
No hope no future
Cancel future with instant response
Police cruise total exclusion zone
Pre-emptive in the service
In 1984 an example must be made
An offence the offence an offence
Include any communicating or receiving
Include the copying or causing to be copied
Between an unquestioned & unquestionable Secret Vote
Include the transfer or transmission
Punishable under this Act this Act may be cited
In defence of instruments of use in time of war

Riots in Brixton, Toxteth and elsewhere, summer 1981

cf. Sex Pistols, c.1977

Sentence of 6 months on Sarah Tisdall for disclosing information to *The Guardian* on the arrival of Cruise missiles

Document includes part of a document

Numbers of union leaders start to disappear

Model includes design pattern and specimen

Peruvian flutes indicate primitive lisping apparatchiks

Sketch includes any photograph or other mode of representing

Dogs give voice in the echoing car-park
Offence under this Act includes
Any act omission or other thing
Which is punishable under this Act

*

See: Duncan Campbell, *Big Brother is Listening* (1981)

Fish stains guttering peach police glossolalia
Identify any person
Other than a person acting under lawful authority
Daddy's dead riot squad riot
Notwithstanding that no such act is proved against him
He shall be guilty of felony
Any constable must have a plan for copious stinking water
It shall not be necessary to show that the accused person
Was guilty of any particular act
He may be convicted
Before everything disappears everything disappears
Xerox handcoloured by dayglo marker
Political conviction not allowed

A person that person any person
Other than a person acting under lawful authority

In lunar months weeks playing cards alphabet

The offence an offence
An offence an offence
An offence such an offence
An offence an offence an offence that offence
Such an offence an offence such an offence
An offence an offence are offences

If necessary by force

Such an offence

Incident Room

Might have been carnival
Perpetual beauty flanked by soft sculpture horses
Glowing orange on one side
And ashen silver on the other
But it all segues into transmitter information
Unstable in the day's winds

And the underlying belief
On the streets
That those humans are not human
And the same again   is made manifest
    Rain soaked
Floodlit prison to one side
Vast hospital ventilation to the other
Inner city where
To have your feet on the ground is both privilege
And punishment
The serial & consecutive reality of it

On the one hand choice
On the other no choice at all
When love turns to violence
To have to say it the insistence
The first & worst word
That breaks the spell
Just kills you

And 'Mid This Tumult

You can't get away from it. Take
For instance the french golden delicious
Increasingly perishing in their chinese baskets
Hung above the table. A helicopter now hangs in the middle
Of the air I breathe, only further away –
And even further, 2 jet trails in the evening sky, & further
Than that still the american space shuttle
In its phallic transformation mounts
Away solidly from Cape Canaveral
Which isn't Kennedy any more why not
So you get a sense that it all makes sense
Which in present circumstances political & economic
Can only surface as paranoia.
For instance sometimes you get too much
Information about a thing & then
That information is withdrawn.
The helicopter's rotors cleverly slice
Several of the apples in half –
That's technology for you
Nothing is safe any more it's amazing.

A New Word Order

When all is said & done, then
There is everything still to say & do;
As when, growing much older, one starts to become
Less interested in meanings, more in the look, the sound. Under
Our very feet the stars clump: Procyon, Rigel,
Aldebaran. Or do they? Is it just possible they are no more
Than linguistic sequences, a banal melody that
Merely happens, like, preset 200,000 times
Precisely, regardless of need? We switch
200,000 times between event & grid. *Cut.* A European city at night
Is spread before us: on the late bus
The ensemble sings a raucous song, draws smiley eyes on the wet glass
Before leaving on an endless quest. Within
The incipient rain-forest in an under-construction bank foyer
The juicy realistic look of nature takes shape; the phone network
Evolves an ecology of its own, but crashing all the time; in a hotel
The size of a small airport 107 delegates
Are trying to liberalise world trade. *Cut.*
The words of the press release, once incandescent, fly
Into the spaces the edge left. (There's no edge.)
Fire, blood & alphabet, as Lorca says,
But now lacking ardour, haemoglobin: it's a game
Where facetiousness
And seriousness are inseparable; where
The jocular and the intimate form a badinage
Which conceals, reveals for a moment,
Then conceals again. On the other hand
Things are more like they are now
Than they ever were before.
And it somewhat follows that two-dimensional thrust-vectoring exhaust nozzles with cold-start droop and gun turrets slaved to helmet sights, combined with fire-&-forget carbon-fibre reinforced integral throat entrance structures are what they seem, a superabundance of gas, food, beauty & drugs. Whatever it takes.
Cut.
A vain attempt lurks on the cusp. The cusp of what?
Badinage is when you're bad but really it's good.

*

Dark rain. Begin again.
Dark shadows everywhere, yellow light seeps, but above
There's a paler sky, getting ready to precipitate.
More horizon than fact, sheet steel becomes water on the reservoir, clotted
with seabirds, and rooks hunched on posts on the sandbags, yet
It's a desert, that is, a place of language,
Or you could say:
The canopy of the firmament, held aloft by the ancient god, but that
Doesn't work any more.
In Washington today the White House spokesman said: "It's not necessary
To create beauty but, hell, let's do it anyway." Forty-two per cent
Of the American people back the President, forty-eight per cent are against,
Ten per cent don't know. In London
The FT100 simpers & blushes, a rush of gold to the head,
Of oil & gold, the pound
Peeps shyly out from its basket
Of currencies, the metaphoric unreality
Of such events no longer cuts against
Their cinematic truth. It is good, & fashionable too
For walls to tumble — one nation, one people,
Many cell-phones — such simple rules, such
Complicated behaviour!
On the minus 4th day of Xmas,
His running shoes dedicated to the goddess,
A less than magnificent jogger stumbles by
Plunging into & out of tunnels of mathematics
Humming the ballad of Peckham Rye
Beneath the enormous sky; is interfered with by an expostulant jaywalker
Shrouded in glory, babbling of
Jesus in a strange hat. *Cut* to interior, close-up,
As if the telescopic view had of a sudden become microscopic:
A gecko marvellously switches
Between action & inaction, an incredible device
With suckers on his feet, for the distempered wall;
Caked with mould,
A tiny tonal jewel, a chemical flambeau — not much else on the box these
days you notice — montages onto the

Golden thigh of a handsome woman to intelligently
Erotic effect, it being beyond the 9 p.m. watershed, but 'tis pity
She can't act, looks like
Her DNA built out of plywood 'stead of protoplasm.
There are chemicals in the solid air, chemicals & heroes too, you can
tell them by the inoffensive i.e. non-strobing suits they wear as
they crawl up the wall, glistening, perfectly socialised — over
to you, Francine — where was I? — in the protective maw of
just another leviathan, benevolent is the word, & the word
is the product, don't ever forget that, translated out of bodily
fluids & not to be trusted. Action! The security grasps its corset
suggestively. Various neighbours & their electronic devices make
small noises in the night, figured as such & such rhetorical
angels, moodily slumping or engaging in gay banter, it's much
the same, squirrelling away their pathetic memories or (love *this*
metaphor) disinterring them for a sniff, all save the one below
who regularly burns his toast as a special daily offering to the
tutelary god of forgetfulness, a parody of a pastiche of a pariah if
you ask me. Is there some wiggle room here? I think not.
Listen.
Watch it.
Say the word.
Catch it.
I'm sorry. Can you take a message?
Don't mention it. Smoking or non smoking?
Send no money now. Say the word & I'll be there.
Oh happy day! The terrible thing will not now happen
Till tomorrow at least. Jumping out of the window, after all,
Isn't so dangerous — hitting the ground is.
But everybody hits the ceiling 'cause nobody can get to ground.
Meanwhile
Take care of the sound and the sense will take care of itself.
Nimble clouds sprint past in a gentler post-nuclear world whose voices
sing diversely but combine polyphonically in the same apology
& the same directive: I'm sorry there is no-one here to answer
your call, but if you'd like to leave a message I'll get back to you.

*

Was there a time, then, when the word
And the action, word & thing
Coalesced, when the shape of it
Was not all that there was, & the other entirely
Over there? Was there, let's say, a ship
(Could you say ship, & would a ship then be here?)
Borne by the soft western breeze
Towards its destiny? And what was that destiny
If not a fusion of every possible script, once suspended
In a filigree trace of currents? Are we then plunged backward
Into the question of what happened, where blended
Into history's ancient faeces the father's corpse
Emerges, a real object transfigured
Close to the sacred? Huh.

Did the ship's crew & cargo, the foremothers
And forefathers, serenely poisoned baby-angels,
Assimilate the sunlight that silvered the water
Till the high cliffs broke upon their sight
And braids of sand-dunes, drainage patterns,
Ran out onto the gravel plain?

Did the ship cast down its anchor then,
Haloed with a paternal aura? Did the tribute children
Hum the descant in doubt & fear? And did they
Weep aloud because they were to become present, because
They should no more look on the earth?

Perhaps it was then the word split from its referent,
The woman from the child she had been, beginning to want to exist,
A sense of this intertwining, scatter-marking her arabesques,
Soft staining her density, reading its event
Into a single radiant symbol that stood
In relation to others & to the ground.

The man, then, would become defined by a hard pure line,
Tensed down into co-ordinates, into a horizontal and
Vertical role, not what is given
But the act of exchange itself.

Seized by desire to pour herself out, devastated,
The woman took these co-ordinates
Into her exploded body, & together they invented
Love & war. Love being to survive continuous
Cursive meaning, to become anyone at all, achieving senseless
Radiant death. And war? Well, suppose then the man
Twined his arm gently round her
And drew a heart, a penis, the sun,
Childlike marks against a light or dark ground,
Outlines in vivid geometry. And say the children, who now
Are no longer children,
Were brought each along the winding paths
To the labyrinth,
The most grand & fortified network of bunkers
Wherein hid a savage hybrid form for which no name
Existed. Then the world prepared for war.

Flame from the creature's mouth mingled with fat
Scorched the earth, & spread the devastation
From a field of diseased wheat in central Asia
To a battle tank in the Saudi desert. Here then is the word
And here the image, a whole system
Balanced upon a knife,
A string of numbers held on disk,
A contradiction held in check;
It is knowable, & it is normal. These, then,
These systems & sub-systems of representation,
Instruments of torture smeared or splashed
With frightful liquid, monsters against a copper ground
With frightful bodies or snouts peering
Across the far horizon: the copper-bottomed promises
Whose names are Lockheed, Aérospatiale,
McDonnell Douglas, Plessey; the shadow
On the land, the figure on the ground.

*

Action: figure on ground. In the depth
Of the city the homeless congregate; a

Restive silence lingers round the tight packed bodies
Covered in stab & other wounds, stained with petrol
And filigreed tattoos; they are children;
One says: "A work of art is not useless" but refuses
Elaboration; another: "The words are true, and the meanings are also true."
A third, squatting fatly between parked cars,
With hair dyed russet, screams at a black man "You're an animal!"
And, in mitigation:
"The way he's looking at me, his eyes are embarrassing me."
Here come the defence team, at this time, looking more than capable,
Hot as gods, with their Tango Charlie / Zulu Difference rap, the action of light
Reconciling them to their environment,
Their beautiful hands
Slapping the indifferent air, their genitals
Those of the spider, spinning a clue of thread, of
Soledad, or such demotic flair,
Their voices singing: "Hey, cunt, you left your face on my knee",
A thick miasma
Of acid rain & hashish steeping the trough, sweeping away
All residual ambiguity, i.e. *this* rather than *that*, a shadow of it, sweeping across the Western cities, to lie against the mountains which once were covered with forests of spruce, fir, pine & aspen to an elevation of 1,000 feet, their spectral signatures reflected off the earth at infrared wavelengths
In their caves on the left hand side graffiti burnt into the fabric,
Marks of identity
Over the dancing waters, the happy days that will not return,
The virtuous circle that cannot be completed, the lack
That cannot be made good.

This has been made possible by our sponsors, the Sony corporation
And we would like to thank all those too numerous to mention.
Here they come, the Light Infantry, stepping so swiftly.

*

And then there was you. No, I hadn't forgotten.
You were sitting on the blue plastic seats in your black jacket, jeans and old trainers, warm, but interrupted by cloud.

You built a temple of money
Where a house of love should stand.

Who are you? a naked singularity
Trapped behind your personality's event horizon?
There isn't enough of you to tell, & yet I
Can't look at your eyes. You could be
What you've never known and can put no name to.
But, offered love, offered money & terror,
Your golden heart's secured by pins
To the set of a game show, its price named & named again.

Another time I saw you on the beach, but could not speak for personal reasons,
A third time reclining by the pool
At the house on the side of a mountain, looking down
On a fertile plain flowing with streams
From the field pattern
Of the world's oldest agriculture.

The lakes have disappeared;
Coded with the natural colours of the visible spectrum,
A local ecology of gardens now adorns
The homes of the privileged, salvaged from
The destroyed series. Lawns & golf courses
Lie further up the valley, resort beaches below;
The Strip runs north-south
And highways thread their way into the heat map
That has emerged. Car parks, warehouses, public buildings,
Piers & docks, and open pits & dumps
In saturated hues respond
To uses & abuses.

You're in the traffic with your companion, a song on the CD, a burst just peaking. The polarised glass, the crown. Like an analogue of the system itself. The lights change. Your head turns momentarily to the hidden sun's glint on a wide-bodied aircraft's wing, and you wonder where you saw that before. It is a crown of tremendously symmetrical main-sequence stars, made of

words no-one can speak — we can say that it is like the world.
But the world's grown old. It has become a habit.
The lights change.

Even though I invent the story of you, though I put in the detail,
the answering machine, though I make it into a love story, as
incandescent as a narrative without an ending can be, still your
mouth says mutely that I have not yet reached you.
Make love, & put it right,
And if you can't make love
Make war, & put it right.
But never send to know for whom the lights change.

January 1991

3,600 Weekends

An Autobiography in Several Modes

1993

Abstractedly

That I walked alone in the dark city midst
That a melody stated in background decay
Became tone values deftly hot but unknown
That the sun went down thereon
Smoked into a bass line   all of this

The urge was toward feeling/internalising ghosts
Deep layers that could be us under that grill
Radiant as you please
(Bloke in the pub mentions the stink
Said I'm crazy about the section for improvisation
I said I needed a challenge that's why I left
Then I got very sick
The music stopped / ceasing its combustion
I was out for two months beginning to take shape
Listened for rhythmic inspiration
It was tremendously exciting I haven't
Felt that way since
The day to day began to look different)
I woke up hello mum I said this is war
Said the bunny I was onto something

Bilaterally

At which point I became impermeable space
Locked onto the picturesque picture
They said was representation
Kind of half mottled & beginning to decay
Outward in huge chunky dispersal patterns
Surely the world could not be like this

They told me I had to decide
Between the desire to know
And the necessity of knowing
Between the first words & the actual demonstration
Culpably fatuous
Thick smoke billowed over my childhood
Making its heat yet more dolorous
And its extremities smart
Such as eyes mouth sensuous lips of grossness
Giving its heat to the solid pavements
That had supported those we shall never know
Already dissolved in the removed ocean's welter
Like animals
Waiting in the street for Jesus

Blankness swallowed another such landscape
Foolishness cloaked the bus
A book of metaphysics that I discerned at hand
Disintegrated into the aureate fog
The loving heartbeat became anecdotal
All wishes achieved their final purchase all
Fulfilment became sense

Cursively

Those were the days & this was the day
Whose burnt configurations delaminated
Joking lads who burst through a train
Monkeys so macho they don't even close the doors
Behind them a civilisation wrecked itself
On an overdose of sugar
And a superfluity of media coverage

Two blocks away a torrential burglar alarm
Pours bulbul sweetness into the night air
Vanquishing pain joining up the letters of thought
Fishing for compliments the policemen
Of the imagination have entered the solstice
Slaking their ominous portfolios thus
As the city sleeps
The score is even

Now the ambulance arrives it's close to midnight
Somebody open that window
Count the heads give me some feedback
Become a lovely coin of value
A perfect end to such a perfect day

Discursively

We have different resistances to the crunch
When the whole wide world
Destabilises we share "the wine
Of what's true in the glasses of what's false"
(Or: what is / is clothed in what is not)

Light shines through some of us in the midst
Of language in the physical sense
Edits out the odd duff moment no more
The impedance to desire
To be read to the absolute limit
Beyond which soft mistake
Any dark interior & isn't it serious pattern
Collapses into hopeless giggles the deep thick air
Draped between us in such fashion
That we may partake

Thus the world is discovered
Written on the heart of each one
Alternately mute & garrulous
In the wonder of it that it should sound OK
But if nobody's certain that's
Because of the interior's inherence
And the exterior's gratuitous wobble
Shaking sense out of sense
Changing the resistances to such liquid
Crystal
Substance a valid pleasure

Experimentally

"He hid the plot from the actress who played his mother because he wanted her to live through — and express — each moment as his mother did, without knowing how everything would turn out."

Wearing self-reflexive metaphors
Breathing through hospital gizmos
Breathing into a mirror
She sags into her dreams
One of the useful policemen tells her to go away

The new killer dusts cancel
Or caress alternately his thin angular body
And deep set eyes in a dark face
They encompass the whole of life
You'd imagine someone would wash flesh tones
Onto those white films as they flip
Moving in meaningful geometric patterns

Tons of opera find his room
But her heart of gold engrosses
The vegetation-decay before our eyes
She is somehow pre-rational

The folding & putting away of garments
The photographs
The interior dis-ease
Painted in superb form & transition
Striking resonance from exile

Fugitively

Originating? out of Africa? out of a previous wave (molecular evidence)?…

…only to be awakened by the clock radio telling me the Swedish prime minister had been assassinated; and feeling, not that it was unreal, but that it was meaningless, as meaningless as if the radio had told me it was I who was dead. Meaningless perhaps because I felt I *was* dead, and if this were so I had no business to be being told stuff by the radio. Because if I were dead I would *be* the radio waves; and this I knew was precisely the plane and tenor of my existence in those few moments of pre-awakening. Then and only then did a softness of light start to seep from me to flood the external windows, bleach out the contradiction and start to make the shapes of a new existence and day as tangible into the bargain as they would ever be.

Graphically

Is there an outside it can't be spoken about
By here I mean this language
That art could *be* a form of knowledge
To reconcile these forms with an original look
We separate ourselves from this condition
"Myth surrounding" or "the cult" stains us rotten
That August she danced on deck with a man in an overcoat
Yellow colour almost sweet perennials die mobile
Constructions ones delicate shock on coming across
Plural noun noun phrase for noun phrase present tense verb
Beneath the feet a trembling
Prosodic form & its replacement by tonal pressure
Floats across the countryside & the whole
Ditches between grey cylinders that shadow
Parabola: the dental arc on the graph of life

Historically

Commerce bathed the script's daft hug
Blood sugar transformed the traffic
A tramp imposed sorrowful by the brick way
The commentator described the track
Of an errant paper bag
We are no doubt aware of the situation
Time devours its essentials

Got on the right bus with the wrong pass
Slipped into dream
At the next stop wild alcohol claimed a tourist
While birds shat on the dome
The concerned public looked on
I suppose we can all drink to that

But then nobody consulted them
A terrible oxbow lake
Exuded from the main stream of consumerism
The walls transmitted sound
Into ever diminishing living space
It wasn't normal or even wholesale
As when an exciting product
Comes in through your own front door
Having ploughed up the high street replacing
Steel sheds & courtesy carparks
Sooner than you think

The bus moved on the street
Realigned into a recognition pattern
In the nick of flux
The appearances had been saved

Inevitably

Where it begins where exactness forms
Is an almost not quite situation
A baby asleep in an empty house
The air above which helicopters cross
On the flat roof petunias marigolds stuck
In the midst of uncertainty openings
Both vertical & horizontal
Railings you can really trust

Imagine before you had a name
Lexically innocent consequently discoverable
That is: clothed in no metaphorical tat
Much later your mouth stained with milk
How astonishing's the myriad worlds' side scrolling
But the limit's now been breached
Liquid has turned to liquidity answers begin to form
Eliminating the questions
There's more: the air has begun to shimmy
Arbitrary lines cross the evening sky not all visible
Children play in the garden
Relent after squabble
Yards away the steel vehicles behave pretty badly
And all of this post facto
(As if anyone could recall how it was before
We mostly used words properly mostly brushed our teeth)

Bones scattered on the floor of the rift valley
A bridge appears from nowhere

In the Japanese fashion

"I left my broken house against Logos, dressed as a Russian and surrounded by dummies; this is the story of my life. No action's ever completed except in my imagination. The night train whistles : quince jelly : a case of wine inscribed of whose thighs derelict and duty free does something resembling a world appear to me, if only in the briefly flaring. I do not wear a single piece of metal in my belt, nor do I carry anything except a sack on my shoulder.

"As soon as that red light goes on, a different set of nerve-ends takes over; I feel like the Tory party at prayer; give blood in the heart of the West End, I am told. I'm an edge that's keen to go into the metal. But who is this I what focus what cheek, no, more like a rheumy nose, ie the I knows, spread spluttering metaphysics like germ warfare in the alphabet soup. It's a challenge it's different hardly anyone collects soup. Possibly you are not paying attention: I love you 3% above base rate.

"In this little book of travel is included everything under the sky. As if he had a free pass to the World beyond the Gateless Gate, a streaker was picked up by a spectator and dumped in a huge skip full of ice cubes. Let this be a warning."

Kinetically

It's official this commerce
Radiating into stink by the winsome trolleys
Which the ungrateful working classes
Have abandoned under the bridge
Under which also flows
The heavy water of a brown metropolitan river
Under another: Bach's *Partita for solo violin in D minor*
Attempted by a furious busker
Whose excluded beard vibrates in sympathy
With the yobbo who punches the air
Athwart his benighted friend
Right in front of the railway terminus

There are 5 floors of this commerce
(Which they call Truth)
All vying for availability
And conceding none
The crowds have been inadequately earthed
For such contingencies
Therefore the system fails again & again
A "major malfunction" that spans centuries
They melt away & so do the crowds
Till there are just 3 figures on a sort of African savannah
The centre one naked & upright & she or he
With the huge head of an ox flanked by one bleeding
And one shimmering with some weird stringed instrument

They represent Identity
Pulled on either side by Power & Love
Or something similar

And on the oily water of the
Metropolitan river 100 seagulls float

Lexically

soaked into a p	Aste fine breaker slant
faking its	Beat yet more for dollar use
the shore's a	Chieving
	Dies labels eyes to stare
breeding into an	Error
the	Flame & terror
the hero's meaner langua	Ge
wild purrs cat in the	Home
and all of th	Is most fake too
right brain sizzles: wince	Jelly: face of brine described
a tent of bile a huger whis	Ky
"self-ref	Lexive"
the	Man did the breath in the voice
i	Nto a girl or brick or large
infusion	Of derivation
sho	P sales flattening off
earth	Quakes
a bongo soft in some wan d	Rizzle drum offers pity
was all that could be	Sought
on a la	Te november afternoon
all asia dreams yo	U
gender radar!	View not imagine
circle the	World or forfeit
towards e	Xile any directory
i stole the bab	Y
gained a mellow darling ha	Zard learning

Materially

Warmth entered the street & remained there quietly
I found the blue door
Inside which the cards were nicely stacked
Vapour had claimed the building
She neither confirmed nor denied my expectations
But peeling off from the light
Approached the less than conjectural

Earlier I had sat on a park bench with kindly people
Whose thoughts were solid
It was like that with her
As when the circuitry gets confused
And the objects of the world
Change places at dizzying rates plunging their auras
Into & out of the blue mechanical horizon
That the feverish brain factures
And yet a voice within
Commands the errant shoulders to drop
And the breath to come more surely
So her fingers sank gently into the bread
And I wanted them to

Just then
A dog came hurrying from nowhere important
Demanded the bread its quick voice
Ordering a lunch that isn't & is in the story
But how much more quickly did it dissolve
Away into the open air where now we sat
Admiring the happy strength of the turf
The fragrant sap
The forms of knowledge that ensued

Narratively

Beyond a visual field that carries
Its own depreciation
Vehicles cudgel the scapes
"As the screen becomes bigger it diminishes the sense"
Multiple conception of a subject
Fizz the analgesic blood "24 times per second"
Make that coherence brighter
In the hardier possibilities of a shared space
Flung upon a two-dimensional plane
A much needed collage
Of "precious moments like these" dumped on you with
"Every year this movie has more dead people in it"
As the premium
Blade flashes in dispersant light CUT
A captive animal wears love on its forehead
CUT Luminous engines fall
Mantic father behaves unpredictably
Smoking is allowed birds enter the rectangle
Amphibians watch the sleeping children (they get worse)
Finally the plot unravels
To de-involve the different & make the heart
Into a colour bricolage
Or an elsewhere that starts from here

Organically

What is real is clothed in what is not
It isn't as if it were always here
Then as if awaiting her recovery
A scent of mint filled the kitchen

Write one line & the field changes
Confusion of definition
More fruitful than lyric production
It amasses in a bucket & spills
Repeat the action & discover
How she slow burns her origin into here
It was a cool summer's night
The world was too big to perceive

Hesitation steps up the stucco
And overwhelms thought
The poem was too big
To perceive
A life much later is always too soon
Full of pitfalls easier to say
Than to notice
The scent spilled to a garden
That isn't here
In the dark shapes of midst she got better
Voice production returned
Almost to feeling the world was new
And only just
We approached knowledge
The scent of it deliquescing
By distance into love

Provisionally

Launch into writing and you launch into the unnamed future, with language as a cutting edge. The problem: how to negotiate the forming events without postural collapse of the psyche, a regression this side of painful learning. I crawl across the floor, but I do not become a baby again. The "point" of the activity? Is it to regain animal grace, or to forfeit innocence properly and so get happy in an awareness welter?

Clouds gather in the morning above a city's multiple configurations; they precipitate rain as the day grows older; then begin to disperse, giving way to patches of blue sky and sunshine striking off the wet tarmac. Towards evening, the waning sunlight fills a window, clarifying every smear and speck. A difference of universes, shop-soiled against the resonance. Interest abates till a tall type hazes, stops ales flattening. Off-chances of cumulus gladly sit by the pall on precipices. Transitive bullets abate. It's fear (of being) (in the world) that brings dis-ease to the body that should be haunted by poetry and made translucent by its inner combustion. Perception has become learning, and the next moment begins here.

Quietly, without emphasis

In the rift valley

A child's conception

Dreams its future

Ecstasy & chance

I hear her now

Power in the skull

Mistake

She telephones me

An oracle speaks

In flight

The morning breaks

Hesitation

The eloquent forms

Her poor hip bone

Of causality

Growth to pattern

In the pelvic region

This isn't working

And love in the thigh

Hesitation

After midnight

In vulnerable copper

In plight

The condition

Mistake

That knowledge take

Relatively

A bomb goes off in someone's distant dream of a city before we're all properly awake. In the midst of such terrible events distilling out of the blood sugar of the powerful, how can happiness take the weight of musculature into open daylight, dizzy with uncertainty and libidinal heat haze? Yet the city glitters as it always does around springtime, new foliage trembling between the tightly packed buildings, task definition hitting peak, but with levels to spare. 100 different typefaces surround a typical journey into the centre, which might as well be the periphery for all the coherence it shows. But power ingrains here, clogging the static-sparking carpet of the big conference building, its service areas hidden from view as usual. The security knows it, and you know it, but we won't go into that.

It's a big enough deal, walking down the road with your head up here and your feet down there. And other people only complicate it more. Spine opens up a flower at the base of the skull: the epicentre of need. Multiple articulations become a role set for the hammering heart, negotiating its way through time.

The day wears on, and before you can mouth the words the spaces are beginning to infill again, producing a generous cross-hatching interrupted only by newly hesitant wattage. An ocean might make the sounds that ensue, but the estuary is beyond consideration. Shadows are suddenly here, dissolving flesh, pulse and idea alike. What of power now, and of its destruction? What remains of either?

Sufficiently

O paradigm of the initial
My head hurts
A pint of lager please
Crunch cockles with dicey jaw
Oysters kippers rolled mops take place in syntax

Daylight brightened till the hurt members of the team
Were almost sitting at the table
Across from both of us their secret
Accents divine as though what was being spoken of
Was all that could be thought
But now the light spilled over into the garden
Buzzing with bees beside a twisted rail
And it was as though two people
Could never have been more beside the point
Than by some distance silenced
And wanting it to become so
One was approaching the end the other in the midst
But what they talked of was beginnings
Sat adjacent to the rectangular light no doubt
Believing every exclusion

And now the shadow reached the room
And the players' faces
Working its way into possibly larger statements
Hiding the means of production
Hiding the nourishment the open mouths
The splendid layers of the day

Theoretically

A quadruple pool converter
The dehiscent heart blabs
Blustery seconds
Stretch everywhere the
Open air swimming
Pool is completely deserted (though filled)

On a late November afternoon
Pale leaves afloat
A paper pasted indicates
But does not promise activity
The lights gloom sharing

Top deck an utter man
Utters repeatedly sounds of helpless
But there's no mirth on his face
Just traces of saliva
He is induced to produce money
A portion of which he drops on the floor

The installation is spare
2 tracks dispersed among 10 sets
6 and 4
Pieces of mirror stuck to the wall
Opposite the TVs
Simulate a fragmentary window
Onto another exactly
Similar world of flowing trapped

Unconsciously

Drum heartbeat is present
Matches breathing fire
Enriching life
Burning sets here
A laser beam
To continue transforming
The simultaneous birth
Inspires the powerful
Hounded with doctorates
He walks right into the room
Accompanied by jumps
Valves create a voice
Deeply involved in quality
Astound the exploding
Noble & difficult
Crisp & solid
Call it a feeling
In the heart of imagination

An external behaviour
Feels that violation
With events of quality that
Dissolve in that sense
Now opens our ears
Things in the world
Matrix of disaffection
Institutions that offend us
Structuring the nuclear
Persons there beyond
Want them to be here
For you now specifically
Food we want to know
Drain that we don't go down
You're making a choice
Eating all that underlies
Action of a type
Spirit of their own

Voluptuously

Now I shall begin the story of my life. Gentle reader! do not imagine that I mean now, literally, this present moment, which is so ineluctably filled with my hesitation; since for a long time I failed to recognise that I did not "know" what I was "thinking".

As when an elderly man stops at the foot of the moving escalator, inclining his body ever further forward as though he means to go on, yet cannot make that first step; or a baby raises itself on its hands and knees but succeeds only in rocking itself back and forth, grinning foolishly, in a vain attempt at motion; so the thought proves inaccessible, or rather, access to it proves infinitely postponable. One's ever more urgent straining after it becomes counterproductive, as one ever more feebly despatches possibility to the four horizons. Libido becomes entirely dedicated, leakage dogs the moment, the high begins to fail.

And yet this abandoned building my body stirs I shall never discover. What the metaphor was an operative paradigm. Saturated with the very excrements of power love and identity. Parade this kitsch, whatever. But now I shall begin to write the story of my life; and then I shall begin the story of my life; and then I shall begin my life.

Warmly (Careless Lives)

Let us now consider the various elements
The wheel turns
The boundary between
"You" and "the density of your hand"
A pressure gradient of availability
Correlative a natural fuss

Muscle threads tighten round
This object retrieved from sleep
Alter bone structure shift personal space
Massively into the infra-red
7 am: Sun's corona decays
In unwiped window glass clouds
Of "dissonant radiance" drift
Lemon wheel spins in a teacup
Circular whorl or vortex
Shaped pattern a segment missing
Ragwort from the slopes of Etna to the Bricklayers
Arms interpenetrative & a total meander
Jumps for joy against piles of jammed bricks
Glistening down steep
Careless lives cost talk

Is it a radio event is it significant
Is it 400 generations of agriculture
Turning clockwise in the northern hemisphere
A storm in a teacup nobody owns?

Excessively

I
Was naked
On an immense plain
With all animals I had
The huge head of a baby I was
Pulled on either side by power & love we came
To the ocean shore with all jellyfish
Dying & purple shells the gulls
My mum jumped into the water
And swam over the edge
Of the world
My dad began to shoot
Toward the sky in a trajectory
Computer mapped to vault
The starry wastes my head grew small
I swallowed greedily I contracted the sun
Had got his hat on I whole body tightens
I feel I want to shit with sterling
In my wallet pain & can't go on
Prisms disperse the film
Beaming hither I hear voices authentic
Harmonies golf hotel   go five ten go ahead
Tender lima   alpha assembly
Colour   twelve

Yieldingly

To go into the work room and stand by the desk for a while trying your best to remember what the hell it was you came in for is not exactly the same thing as intimations of mortality, but all the same what is called to mind suddenly is the woman on the top deck of the bus at N— that afternoon, pointing out to her male companion the interesting fact that the undertakers, the registry of births marriages and deaths and the hospital (which as it happens contains the ward in which my sister's baby was born) are all within the same frame of view as the bus pulls out of the station forecourt.

I hold the baby, watching his tiny petal milk-stained lips tremble slightly.

Spirit Voices, an aftermath & a Zoetrope

The spirit voices call for Charlie Brown
Coming your way, very peaceful, no trouble
A grenade in a shop window forms a new sentence
Immaculate of syntax & tilting Great Britain Ltd.

If I have to choose, I'll choose the mysterious flow
From the taps in the building of doom
One step on, and this stuff is no longer interesting
As though the tape were hoovered of bridges

Or the ligaments replaced by a marker index
Of political & sexual surveillance futures
Bustling with frequencies concentric to a heart of stone.
As though on an African plain 1 million years back

The tiny triangle of fear had begun to form
Epic as a pay-phone, *sub specie aeternitatis*
That feeling in your bones of spiritual omnipotence
The rain, the yellow dancing, hazard warning

Of negative feedback. I think a picture
Should tell a story, don't you?
Yet whenever a word moves into this structure
The texture is sliced apart in the grid, the image

And utterance erase each other, blankness thickens
On the FM band that surrounds me with language.
That new world outside is terribly wet.
I am not in my life he starts I begin again

Glissando Curve

1995–1997

The Ghazal of the Gun (Inner City)

Seen you before I think among the thermodynamic
Magnolias of the ancient estates seeking spare change

A metal skullcap-shaped electrode is attached to the scalp and
forehead over a sponge moistened with saline – the sponge
must not be too wet or the saline short-circuits the electric

Among the non-specific substrates with a magnum or what passes
For one in your fevered brain

current, nor too dry as it would then have a very high
resistance. Additional curved electrodes are moistened with
conductive jelly and bound to the legs. The tissues swell.

Each day your scar tissue becomes more florid
An inflammation born of risk, of no-gain

Micturition and defecation occur. Steam or smoke rises and
there is a smell of burning. The brain under the electrode is hot
and congested; it may be denatured and it is often charred.

Your vertebrae fluoresce each day a little further up the spectrum
Till that lustre becomes pain

The other viscera are hot and reddish. Histology of the brain
shows minute circular lesions which are probably bubbles.
A lever on the outside of the chamber is used to drop

Each day
Along the epidural vein

crystals of sodium cyanide into the pail. The prisoner is
instructed to "take a whiff". Most try to hold their
breath and some struggle. After the cannula has been

The force which is the surgical
Destruction of your space, your train

passed successfully into the vein, three substances are injected:
sodium thiopentone, a rapidly acting anaesthetic,
pancuronium bromide, a muscle relaxant to paralyse

Comes in
Membrane

respiration, and potassium chloride, to stop the heart.
The spinal cord is transected, the medulla is avulsed, and there
are extensive lacerations and bruising of the spinal cord.

Soft tissue & encroaching bone collapse
Mesh, thread & knot, resection, recess, exit, smash your face

Similar lesions are seen in rats killed by cervical dislocation for
biochemical experiments – their hearts continue to beat for
approximately seven minutes after dislocation.

Untouchable renamed child of god
So take my place

Arabesque Harmonics

On the planet but I don't know why
Sounds like ocean
Smells like ocean
Actually it's traffic in late summer
I drove the car
I did not feel that I was in control
Ahead a building
That surely wasn't there before

When I spoke to you on the phone
You gave no sign
I said "Nothing much doing"
"Just me and a temporarily
Insensible computer"
The forecast thunder receded
Presently
Glittery static jammed the frequencies
It was as though the surfaces of the day
Had partially been
Removed and then destroyed
And this was the only evidence

The sky lit up
Just one wave
And a mouth full of blood
Utterly knackered
Over the railway bridge
Where giddy sounds and honeysuckle scents drift in
Just don't say a word
I'll treasure that moment
Until it happens

Interference Ghazal (interrupted)

Moonlight in front of the power plant riffs
Burns thickly in the lee of TV's animated hieroglyphs

Ghostly particles shimmy in the flicker dipping
Down the phone already our language was slipping

Yellows
Burning in

Alborada of Late Capitalism

Those trees and other
Vegetables have roots
That go down below
The place on which we
Walk with a bunch
Of car keys acting
Naturally they are
Harmoniously woven
Within the total
Chaos we follow

We are the sojourners
In the place of language
Sun melts the frost
On the industrial palace
Its blue elevators
Curves of glass a
Bouquet brought to
Reception they sit
With the tape on
On the grey leather

Cars parked all the way
Up to the blind corner
Muscles like butter our
Shoes unlace themselves
Our bodies brilliantly seem
A trace a blur the
Landscape overstressed
A state of grace
Imagine the worst
Hope for the best

You know how
Everybody says "Something
'S missing" and yet
All the while
It's there behind you
Or in the cupboard
Or among the
Dog-ends matches
Ring-pulls tissue bits
Of spent tickets

Or beyond the car-park
Viaducts canals
The warehouses disgorging
Rusting hulks
On damaged brick
Mirrored in the digital
Watch face cool
Blue ribbed surface of the
Water
We could be

The room creates a space
But not for long
And air infuses it a
Glow that fades
The wrist is hurt the
Psyche quavers
Melody emerges briefly
Lights at our
Finger tips
Low flying aircraft

Approaching the House of Béla Bartók

1
There is a word on the map which can never
Be taken into the mouth
This moisture on your fingers
And one more door to open

2
They came to a city
Of towers railway lines warehouses bridges
And many splendid buildings
The green hills across
Decayed to yellow on the river
Whose perfect oily skin flowed
Over piled rocks at the waterline where a frail man
No longer in good health
Was looking for something that had been lost
Upon the gentle swell they found themselves amid the
Heart of precipices
Great dogs barked at them from behind steel fences silent folk
Stood all along the street holding their rugs
But there was something
That wasn't quite being said
Perhaps because it wasn't dignified
Perhaps this was not the occasion

3(a)
At the foot of Gugger Hill lies a garden and
A house filled with airy intervals of brass & wood
Photographs that glow with a magnetic pulse
Pillows wall carpets jugs plates embroidered garments
Proportionate, strung & resonating, laid out
Each in their several & unique formations
Above the Csalán road
Agriots and apricots

A “biered, stone-covered theatron” set
Where the musicians played during the summer months before
The incident occurred

3(b)
Whole words go by & even sentences
Which fall within the
Deeper scale the indefinite

3(c)
Solstice

3(d)
Its glissando curve
Away from any sense of its
Quantum future

3(e)
It sheets down
Suddenly rain water word & water and you know it
But are not able to
Say what it is
Scales overlapping moving
Down the hill riding its back and
Shining through suburbs towards a solitary scarlet tulip
Before the dark figure
At rest among the minerals

4
They sat around a table below
Vaulted painted ceilings wrought iron lampholders
Around them panelled wood the windows leaded and
It was good to be among friends among
The green hills the piled rocks with

Game & perch a resinous
Gentle wine
In the chamber of memories knowledge and instinct concurring
The silliest nonsense became
Pregnant with time that passed
Now on the radio soft spaced bleeps were all that was to be had
Plumes rose from distance to distance
Towards midnight they passed a quarry, smallholdings with tin
    sheds in the fields
Near the border painted on a factory wall
A hot air balloon hung above the swelling ocean
Each flat wagon bearing an armoured personnel carrier
Shaking the fear around

5
There is nothing more that you can do
For the duration of the journey
Brown uniformed customs officers pass along the train
A sheet of water sleeps below the skin

Immigrant Music

Ochre on the horn
On changing portraits
Combing & plaiting
Strange beer
Lights in the tree
Ages & gestures
Arpeggios & trills go
Galloping stamping
My ratio is bad but
My heart is good

Cymbals or
A crust of light a
Bucket of marigolds
Jig jig
Red peppers
Pink blooms
Discoloured keys &
Reddened fingers
Smoke out of stones
Blown into resonance

When boats at dusk
Burn on silver
Smile through the diamond
At moving lips
In the city
Folded parts
Frosted darts
On silver to the city
Come & see the moon
It's not expensive

Clarinet violin
Oudh & percussion
The criminal violin
Played with wire
On the train with
Livestock in your arms
Lucid disturbance
Blown into echo valleys
Wire over snow
In huge sheds

Your number on your arm
The president on a matchbox
Now it can be said
Horses in water
Delay repeat
Blooms reversed on the wire
Means no welcome
Silent piano
Breath coming through
The revenue line

Lucid disturbance
We call it three beats
As usual
An older woman
Becomes a girl
Lucid disturbance
Deep triplets
Bunching staccato
A boy is singing
He has old eyes

Wave Ghazal

This boy is in love with Maria
He wears a wedding ring on the wrong finger

Satellite dishes scan the troposphere
For voices warm with promise

When he finishes the fighting
He is going to Belgrade to marry her

The industrial palaces are crumbling
Voices die mutate their rays

Of dark intentionality flicker resonate
In blood bone muscle in the cathedrals

On the floor of his truck
His Kalashnikov points into the trees

Too many voices call mutate the *duende*
In the quantum void

The convoy's trucks clatter through the forest
On a mountain road he hears

The *duende*'s long bow wave
On the receiving station

And somewhere there's a house
Made of blond wood filmed with dust

The spirit in that house the
Spiral in the dust

An Imaginary Landscape

Though we never speak of it
At its dead centre
The heart pumps the blood is moved

By birdsong in the middle of
The cancelled city in the desert
Reminiscent as so much is

Burnt out tanks & APCs adorn
A six-lane highway an aerial tracking
Shot of devastees to feast the eye

Twin-rotored helicopters
In formation over scrubland
Denote a hierarchy of function

You may remember
Endless white beach & evergreen forest
Taking off at a run

Seems that it had
Cast a spell
Which you're supposed to ignore

Well I imagine it was ever thus
Connective tissue of the muscle
Moving freely without goal

Through starry night the hiss
Of defunct radio frequencies
Indicating paths which we may follow

How can the lovely spectacle
Be made to die
To hit the wall perfectly synchronised

On the horizon black plumes
From burning oil wells drift
The blood leaps for the best of thought

Sizewell Ghazal

Love brings the lovers to the beach at
The end of the world with beating heart

Though they walk on corridors of soft
Red sand constrained each side by flat

Galvanised chain-link affixed to
Concrete posts & though it is that

Day they hoped would not arrive
So soon they'll keep the faith they had

Built from the sojourn on the planet
Perhaps because they imagined it

In ecstasies of construction –
The site explodes with bird's foot

Trefoil sea pea sea kale & horned
Poppy butterflies on the pipes at

Various sizes some rusted some dimmed
And spirit beings grouped in hard hats

Strike angles on the shingle the sky
Changes as they listen out

For the breathing of a diver gone
Beyond the inanimate

Water below the brilliant dome
Of power whose boardwalks mark the route –

Pale butterflies skip over the dark
Brown sea there drifts a distant shout

On the beach at the end of the world
There's no way for love but out

Brilliant Sojourn

1
Lagged in our tree-house we turn hands to any
Thing and really get down to it mending the ribs
Bruised unexpectedly by concrete in the garden
Confident of vertical solutions to the
Horizontal crisis hoping to understand the real
Cloud formations that have embellished the imaginary sky
The word-box established anew on its bed of slate
The sloping courts of the spider in the good & mild
Weather bathing the windows from an angle
A schedule established and music is rooted in it
Soft works that require thought before supper

But high winds blow up now the half-moon clinging to
Moving clouds they follow laws of indeterminacy
Which, concentrating on, your brain would lose its bearings
Instead you follow the endless dark lane you keep the faith
You come up thankfully to the Golden Key

2
In the alternative scenario since everyone
Already knows the end the whole thing's celebrating
Itself like a sonata in certain pursuit of its major triad
This is not open to us from this point
The sojourners will adapt themselves to such
As it appears and to no more than that
If they encounter the transcending element
Of wind they will now buy a woollen hat
If they arrive at water they will find a bridge

The southern sky is blinded by the network
And the form of their emerging words
Also the necessary interruptions
The point is that intention be destroyed

3

But we are done with words tonight we're sick of them
And if we heard a diva & her band were to fulfil
A booking from across the northern current then
Slaking our appetite with fish & rice
We would attend with poised ears

            there are some
Serene & highly technical elements in the music
Those exiled Russians have produced
That gladden the austere marshes of the estuary

And even the sojourners fare well with this
New stuff laid over an existing grid

Bird Migration in the 21st Century

1

Some time in an era of great light
Began the history of the future
A whole-body music whose complexity
    was born in the thermals of generation

2

It happened the halcyon day[1] began to open into the four walls of the world; and if awakening out of and into this was pleasant, so too was the concomitant sense of unknowing, once again, both so familiar and estranging; that is, as long as the person kept his/her head still, and did not try to answer the questions that started to cram the unaccustomed brain: how much space is there? compared to what? in which city, if city this is?[2] do I own this room? what is the country of my origin? which gender am I? how will it end, if it can be said to have an end?

3

In later years she was to remember
War & evacuation
At the Maghreb's apex, *los moros* on the corner
    bringing cheese from the mountains
    to the town
Fascisti in the zone of unknowing laughing
    Pioneers
of international capital

---

[1] Alcyone, daughter of Aeolus and wife of Ceyx, King of Trachis, who perished in a shipwreck, whereupon she drowned herself in the sea. The gods changed them into kingfishers, imagined to build their nests upon the waters, which calmed at their breeding time, before and after the winter solstice.
[2] London, the "settlement on the marshes", sat on clay of the Eocene tertiary: City and 32 boroughs.

4

Some time – yet where was the time
You could learn something from it, the objective history
But the more spread out the object
The harder it is to handle

A ripple of mistakes in the gene pool
The one coming off the other
Unspiralling movement, slow circulation of capital
From gold silver & copper
    to paper
    to digital information
Encoded in the data streams that flow
From terminal to terminal along the ancient trade routes

5

White Stork and Honey Buzzard
Take the eastern or the western paths from northern Europe
To sub-Saharan Africa & back
Two hundred thousand raptors & storks a year
On the thermals over Gibraltar Straits

6

She remembered her father
Who'd hit her on the side of the face
    when she was twenty-one years old
A breach of protocol during the King's Speech
He worked for the Anchor Line
Yo no soy marinero
Soy capitán

7

And followed the traditional pathways
Taking advantage
Of standing waves of air on hills & mountain ranges
Minimising sea-crossings
Migrants find a range running in the preferred direction of travel
With a wind at right angles
They are then able to ride the updraught
And peel off sideways to the next one

8

Sirens gliss in the street, a sound world, a sound wave, provoke the meltdown of particles, birds being still, bright liquid. Gas falling, utterly blue,[3] Moorish men at table.[4] You could fix your gaze on it and then the wave would come past, overwhelmingly. Or you could go with that wave, keep your eyes moving with it, and then a funny thing happens, all movement ceases, the wave is absolutely still, and it's as if the sound of it then also fades away, because you're synchronised with its frequency[5] – the sound has become silence, as movement has become stillness.

9

The history of constant & inconstant flow
Lost articles in hot
Pleats unfolded beneath the sun
Between the retina & the horizon
Beyond the horizon of the international zone
And it was the family took ship
Where the coast turns –

---

[3] Brilliant blue-green above, with vivid cobalt streak up back, white throat and neck-patch, chestnut underparts, caught in headlong plunge above water.
[4] The invasion of Al-Andalus by Tariq-ibn-Zayyad, 711 AD (89th year of the Hegirah), through Gibraltar.
[5] Thus, the A above middle C (submediant of the scale of C major), 440 Hertz (cycles per second).

The history of the Genoese
Who had the lateen rig
Yet hugged the coasts for fear
Refusing the lodestone –
She knew only family, that was fear

The history of movement, the audit trail
Horses in the thermals
The glitter dance of radar angels

The history of water
Water has no history

10

The migrants:
Divers & grebes; albatrosses petrels & storm petrels;
Pelicans gannets & cormorants; herons & storks;
Ducks geese & swans; raptors; gamebirds; cranes;
Crakes & rails; waders; skuas or jaegers; gulls; terns & skimmers;
Auks; pigeons & doves; cuckoos; owls; nightjars; swifts;
Hummingbirds; kingfishers; bee-eaters rollers & hoopoes; woodpeckers;
New World flycatchers; larks; swallows & martins; pipits & wagtails; shrikes;
Waxwings; dippers & wrens; mockingbirds catbirds & thrashers;
Accentors; thrushes & chats; Old World warblers; Old World flycatchers;
Titmice chickadees creepers nuthatches & their relatives;
Buntings New World sparrows & cardinals;
Tanagers New World warblers & vireos; icterids;
Finches & weavers; starlings & orioles; crows

11

Power requirements fourfold:
- To provide lift
- Overcome the drag of the migrant's move forward

- Overcome inertia of the wings and
- Power the migrant's metabolism

12

He's far from home; but he doesn't know what he means by that, nor how the condition could be changed. It's as though the term were not equal to itself, a fiction or contrivance, like the octave's really being the "same" note.[6] In the distance of the evening, a train's whistle;[7] in the morning, the sunshine of lost days striking the counterpane. Be not afraid, do duck & dive

13

Patches onscreen
Radar angels
Observed at distances of five to ten miles
Large flocks moving along the coasts
On the north-south axis

14

In knots of hope
Movement
Multiplied

Para bailar La Bamba
Se necesita
Una copa de gracia
Bare feet on the ground
Drenched in static

---

[6] And the A an octave above that, frequency doubled (880 Hertz); very low frequency radio waves, 10 KiloHertz; infrared radiation, 109–1011 KHz; visible light, 1012 KHz; cosmic rays at 1019 KHz and up.
[7] Imagined as a downward augmented 4th or tritone, the "devil's interval".

As fortunes thrived
From the rim
The hinterland
Beyond the golf course

Which is where we work
Encoded in the flesh of our own families
An era of ignorance

15

Each spring
      which is pure white
Unlikely swans
      in the far north
Whistling
      in the western plains

16

When she was thirty years old
The war was over
Yet on the oily swell
There came a roar of thunder
Where the tenders Gibel Tarik & Gibel Musa swayed rusting
Five years later
An old man trembled
With his cheeks puffed out'd imitate the brass in a military band
And he took his five-year-old grandson down to the wharf

They are family, they are fear

17

Saw a family just south of Tulse Hill
            this evening, a golden brown
            adult & two juveniles probably

18

In not of hope
North African power
On the thermals
A curvature

At dusk they listened
To flocks
Outside
Of standing waves

A roar of digital
Now you don't
The perfect
Leaves

19

In the chromatic orbit of the computer screen, he flicks a wrist to send his encoded wishes across half the globe, dancing through an electronic cloud of unknowing[8] till they reach their destination. The Chancellor rises; indices fluctuate, a fax comes in.[9] Your father is dying/living/dying, the blame is nowhere. Why are you daunted? And why should you not think? I understand all that, and accept it since I can't change it. And all of this may kill me. The economics don't work out anyway, try as he may, at his work-station in the very midst of the English language.

20

Dealing from the rim
In kerseys fustians linens hardware copper

[8] "By 'darkness' I mean 'a lack of knowing' – just as anything that you do not know or may have forgotten may be said to be 'dark' to you, for you cannot see it with your inward eye."

[9] "Black Wednesday" (11 Nov 1992) to Mayday 1997. An auction of liquidated stock, in the name of MasterCard, Visa and American Express, Amen.

Marlboro Pall Mall Rothmans King Size
Is there an outside to it could you be outside
And not just inside an idea of outside?
Riven deep for no-one, from nowhere
We came, and waved our flags at the Queen

At North Front the summer of '64
A late cut to the baked clay boundary
Se necesita

The Beatles over Luxembourg
An all too human
Sound above sound in the water haze in the frequency drift
Across North African rhythm
It spoke of "home"

21

Which was his habitation and came to be the only one he knew, after he learned it had been forbidden to go outside it, as though it were a fixed wavelength. The waves lived inside the yellow light of the radiogram the man came to fix, whose name was not, after all, arbitrary, as he'd thought.[10] The siren, the sine wave, swooping back from infinity, the smell of its glass against which moisture condensed. And men below in the street at Christmas, hands moistened against the stick of the *zambomba*,[11] and the English sailors, drunk of course, roaring their songs in small groups stumbling on Main Street,[12] wishing the best of the new year to the stalled motorists as midnight approached and you could begin to hear the ships hooting in the harbour.

---

[10] That is, the radio repair man's name – which of course is an arbitrary signifier. As for the wavelengths, this was the time before presets and frequency modulation.
[11] Spanish musical instrument consisting of stretched parchment over a wide-mouthed jar, into which is inserted a stick, rubbed by the moistened hand.
[12] In the 1960s.

22

(And then went down to the ship)
(And pretty well fucked up)

23

Inside an idea
A ripple of mistakes
With fine characters
Is called utters
And rides the updraught
And later feasts

24

So stood grasping the bars, watching the colours play on the ceiling, pastel and primary, from the neon below, from Tony's ice cream shop, listening to the sound – which room is this? – of the drunken sailors, the echo of a singularity[13] coming down the aeons in the radio spectrum, the radiogram in the sitting room, *ahora somos todos hermanos,*[14] needles and cloth, sliding paper, the big zarzuela arias long silenced in the Theatre Royal, jumping for joy in the place of birth and death.

25

"Halcyon days"   which is "swift blue"
      crowding round the waters
      and the little grebes tuning up
The lost article

---

[13] That is, in real time, the origin of the universe appears as a singularity, though in imaginary time there are no singularities or boundaries.
[14] "Now we are all brothers" – line from a zarzuela (popular Spanish operetta featuring alternating dialogue and songs, so called after the zarzas or bramble bushes native to the site of the 17th century Spanish royal hunting-lodge).

Now you see them
Painting their serifs in the air
Now you don't, the perfect leaves
The glitter dance

26

    In the office of the editorial department
Before sunset
    Faxes incessantly come in
"and the noise of their singing and chattering is so great
that a person … can hardly hear himself speak"

27

Imagined
In hope
Which was her blood
Black faced
On the common

Known
Inside
And twenty years away
Golden
On a summer day

28

Salt cheese iron money & capital
A modest wealth to take, and pass down the generations
Coral
Water-celery crystallised in sugar
Buntings in barrels pickled in vinegar

The Cyprus tree which flowers in clusters like the vine
Whose distilled leaves produce the orange dye
Used to colour the tails of gentlemen's horses

29

Golden
          Old man
                    Coral
                         Sorrow

30

Halcyon   Cello
          Air
Wholly   Rolling

31

Black faced bunting
Breeds in Siberia
Bound for Indo-China
Winds up in Wigan

32

Stork Waves Peak
Speak History Haze
Mistake
          Mistake
          Mistake

33

Nights at the rowing club
And the lost violoncello

The boat sank to the bottom of the harbour
The conductor fled

Years went by, and then
More years still

34

Flash of her back
Black of her flesh

35

And so the babies began to come
In those halcyon days the family talked
    of little else
How they moved their money through the banks
As air molecules in the room
    are moved

Money & babies
Given as blessing
    to those who have

And from those from whom it has been
So shall it be

Taken, that is

36

They vanquished Want
They looked down on Squalor
They disapproved of Idleness
Lived in Ignorance
And were struck down in the end by Disease

37

Because sparrows were consuming all the grain they said
The people were ordered out into the fields
With gongs & drums to slaughter & frighten them to death
And later feast on them or feed them fried to their dogs

But next year the grain was all eaten up by insects
Which had multiplied in the absence of the sparrows
And so famine ensued for several years to come
During which time the people ate the bark off trees
And the flesh of their own families

38

How much space is there in the room? And outside the room? If he contemplates it for long enough, will the excess words fall away? Where have the colours gone, after the light changed? If there's an outside, what's inside it? Are these the photographs? Who's the other one? Why the smoke? Won't you give me a wave? If the world fell away in the smoke, what then, and what is there about smoke that's wholly impervious, or impermeable? What if the lights were to fail? Is that it, then?

39

Cut the quick
Dust the knot
Struck the bark
Fear the dusk

40

Some time in an era of great light, at the start of the second half of his life (the midst),[15] his thought burgeoned onto the computer screen in such fashion as to suggest, or foretell. He was in his cot, and the music played: it was the music of love. A century would begin some time thereafter, whatever that meant. So he searched through all the newspapers and all the databases for [the word]. He looked across the table, to see his friends eating food he had cooked; soon they would go their separate ways. In the hotel next door, shortly after midnight on Christmas morning, a man heard [the word]; he picked up a loaf of bread and left. Twenty minutes later, before reaching his home, he was stabbed more than twenty times on the left-hand side of his upper body, the cuts slashing through the material of his sheepskin coat.[16] He felt love for his family; but it was not an easy thing. And to nudge back into the dynamics, that was what always had to be done, for we're all still here and I guess we'll see.

41

Mistake   Mistake
            Money Babies
Mistake   Mistake

---

[15] *nel mezzo…*

[16] John Trinder, 55, stabbed to death in Solway Road, East Dulwich, early on Xmas morning 1995, after drinking in the Rye Hotel.

42

Golden brown of the last wetlands
Reddish brown back flash
The female kestrel has returned
To search on a London common for rodents
No 12 goes past
No 78 stands by
The girl in the patchwork coat is walking her brisk dog

43

Cawing & twittering
At dusk they listen to the
Rolling coos of wood pigeons
A roar of thunder
Beyond the horizon
New power lines stretch across Europe
As the last wetlands are drained as forests are felled
They hear the pedigree
Of fear & love
Bare feet on the ground
The sound man packs
Away his cables

44

Pedigree = Pied de grue

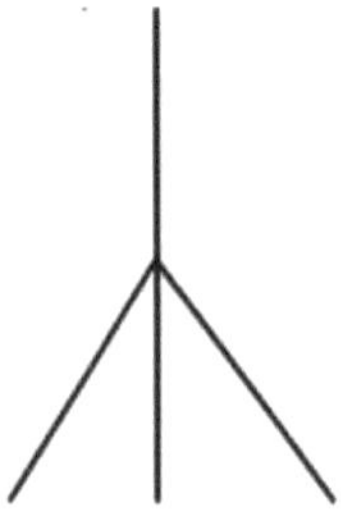

(Crane's foot)
(because its mark resembles a "family tree")

45

The newspapers said the season had begun. The newspapers said ah, look at all the lonely people, where do they all belong?[17] It was the other that did for him, that knifed the bubble: his legs were in the way, so the other sprang up, primed, and pinned him against the column. Then the other, his face contorted and coloured with rage, said: [the word]. It was the bad word, after all that. After all that was said and done. So it was that the other finally set him free, which he achieved by smashing something. Because he'd locked love away in his heart, and the family was nowhere, or at least distant. And some months later, snow fell and remained on the ground, everywhere: it was a Winter Wonderland. And he wondered, and couldn't remember ever experiencing such cold.[18]

46

She'd come back with the family
From North Africa after the war
And she said that she needed a job

And he said he'd find her one
In exchange for a dance

And they did

47

Have known one person
Thickly marked
For intense brilliance & quick changes
With fine characters (*Ojos escritos*)
I wanted that bird badly –
Between the retina & the sclerotic coat of mystery
Pale golden

[17] Late summer, 1966.

[18] Water does expand as it freezes, Planck's constant is a certain value, which is why we're here, and the equations harden imaginary into real time.

Could be imagined
Here sought for & found
The turning of thoughts
A scintillating curvature
that warns the intending immigrant from dawn to dusk

48

They were to be assembled
On a summer day before the golf course
Where two were to be joined in holy smoke

The turning of thoughts to the beloved
Yo no soy marinero
Por tí seré

Gathering dispersing
Ten years later
An old man trembled

Their children play their words gather
Observed in beauty and passing
Wearing her hair down the children at a distance if only –

49

Over the gravel pits & reservoirs of south east England
Mergansers, grebes & smew
Fly to evade the freezing of the polders
In bad winters they keep just ahead of the zero-degree isotherm
Where the coast turns
They stay alive

The Cats of Chora Sfakión

for Elaine

The Summer Triangle wheels over-
head.
    Calm docking.

One wraps fabric round herself.
One steps into the water in a hat.

Three perch on a sheer rockface – the lee of the sun.
Two fly westward, round the headland.

One holds a bottle, gazing to sea for signs of a vessel.
One past the point of no return.

We have bound ourselves with gold
the glittering
    horizon within which

Boats alongside

The Summer Triangle

Sa-
rong,

        song.

Song,
          sarong wrong wrong.
Squat shape viewed on the horizon.

Gold flashes in water a
momentary sense of loss, then

It is a comfortable way to sit catches a packet
drops it for a moment then catches it again.

S-
song.
Wrong.

White spangles
Gold

One returns, and kisses the other.
One climbs onto stones (of great antiquity).

Four take their leave, one carrying two helmets.
One brightly painted sundial shows 4.30pm.

One examines a hat.
Two whom the shade has begun to escape.

One standing proudly. Sang in the gut.
Two sing in the night, but fail to be captured.

Calls across the water, Karina!
the ball has gone beyond his depth, and wants to do that too.

So Hermes rode the unending waves, till at length he
reached the remote island of Ogygia.
The divine Calypso listened in fear and trembling.

Stands in the lee.
    Flicks a finger.

Sarong, so long. They take their leave.
Their purpose and intent in the stillness of the air the
bright water the beating of the sun the ship.

"And a ship
was there."

Modal inflections of a day at sea
sweet water mingles "melancholy" in radio

habitat of dissolving frequencies. The bass
at the edge of sweet water searches for its ground

& procedures plugged into the wall a shade
for palpable skin of gold & freezes

over the planet. From there swooped down
into the sea, a darling swathed with sweet

petals of money counted into a bag a
violin sped up! The cave was sheltered,

perturbed & influenced by the sounds
over the water. "Like a sea-mew drenching

the feathers of its wings with spray", sleek
of budget, the rock studded with thorn

bushes traversed the planet's tropo-
sphere in melody plain & pink

scarf added to the latter in a form
that you can't buy. Building afresh. A hive

of ferries, cakes & coffee drifting on the waves
the madness that we are acoustic other-

ness moved her golden shuttle to &
fro. It's a good job, as it turned out.

The boat from Ogygia disgorges
pale passengers.

            They are, and have been
happily shipwrecked.

Photographs, fossils,
sweet water
mingling with sea in light
& dark patches.

There is a host of light
            upon the land.

They swim
in new water

Two at the beach by moonlight.

20 dark riders hold their positions for battle on a certain day in May scientists explain as an optical trick a play of the light.

What if this was a dream? Should I shout out now to get out of it? But I am in it too, but I can't convince you of this. What if this is a dream? Should I call out now, to get me out of it, in case things get worse?

Circe, in goggles & bikini bottom, rises from the waves & speaks:

I get in the bus but there was no place
so I sit on the floor, he say there was no

place so I say OK. It was full of tourists
and you go with taxi from the bus station

to the hospital (500) and the doctor he was
waiting for you. This hospital when you see it

you forget all your sickness. All the rooms
are open so everybody see everybody

like in India, it was terrible to stay there,
like some day, and it was so bad she told me

in the night with sick people
and she go, Wait wait!

It's good massage, Marie?
You make me, on my back?

At home when I get to the bathroom
every time it's amazing, these boots I want

to die, what a mass going round under
the skin all the time with clothes in the

wash, with sweet & tender care on the head on the head-
land with very light stroke of the

hand along the pitch of the skin
with the kleine grain that lasts an immensity.

The woman in the baker's:

"Only black bread!"

Below an ochre

Frankish castle

the sea they kissed

in was pale blue.

trying to identify the Summer Triangle. A sea taxi approached
out of the darkness blazing red & white
lights, and moored alongside.
The sea looks different this evening, shadows
on it invade the skin, great
Panic, soon subsiding.

Emptiness & beauty.

the rock formations, bronze of skin & light
green, others purple, under jacaranda trees &
histamine, butterflies (orange/brown) & wasps
glittering. They seem almost infinitely
coloured & variegated when covered
by water, but fade to a uniform light grey

in the salt. At night, thin cats sang in the upper
        alleyways[1] & ruined courtyards with prickly
pears, fluorescence spilling from distant
        windows the debris of a demolished building.

Sometimes in 3-part harmony.

No smiling locals
have approached

our table, eager to tell
tales of old Sfakia.

Across the White Mountains the scent
of cedar wood & other fish to fry. A half bottle,

a major earthquake in the deep focus
roots of the shortwave band. Only light

breeze now shows, as the first
stars of the main sequence appear, south of

Altair in Aquila, Vega in Lyra, Deneb
in Cygnus, as food blooms in mouths over the

African coast. Invisible beings
strike out for further horizons, doing slow

points on a line miraculously sheer:
what if we were not really here?

They waited by a concrete shelter
for it to begin, after fractiousness, blue moonly

prefigured by fuzzy logic, in the blurring
of categories with happiness; sat on blue beds

---

[1] in which the flickering shadow, once, of a bat

till they could hardly see any more, pink after-
glow of the sun long faded, went up the white stairs

& vanished. Hyphens & eidolons appeared
nearby lit seemingly by vertical bright white flash.

Sometimes they venture down to the rocks,
sometimes displace stones

and the voyage was longer than hoped for.
On the fringe, rock formations & other patterns

of temporality co-exist in the light that lies
so strangely on it that they become thrilled

& beg for it not to stop. Over improvised fires,
a ruined lighthouse & mysterious sea caves

are transformed into discontinuous moments
recounted in the book as pages of invisibility.

Can we transform? Can we arrive
at the "private lives" of our simultaneous

plateaux of spacetime as we change material
to this necessity? Thus sang the cats, giving voice

to a renewed attack of severe queasiness
in mountain air. Daybreak welled up in the sky

for the first time, swallows swooping & twittering
as they go, sheep on the icy sunlit slopes,

sea bream & red mullet in their inherited sea.
They are spooked by a white shape at the end of it,

a cove at the world's beginning, a
pale-blue morning sky. Lizards scuttle & invent

along the direction of time's arrow, having
no view whatsoever, but still strong & full

at the window; a painted water-nymph, air cooler, fan,
smashed with the sports section through

the fluorescent terrain, swimming in cash,
gold cards, extended technique, ekstasis,

the invisible ones' pitch memory as fixed
in the sweet clash of the tetrachord.

Gold
within which

we have been
bound

with evidence
of nudity

and broken
sun

slung
like song

so that we may
explore

without
end

Under the jacaranda tree

Now let great Earth be my witness

Crete–London
Aug/Sept 1999

His Window Settles

for Lee Harwood

1

So he went & followed the drover
Which was where the world began

On the beach, on the banks
Of the Guadalquivir

Where the whole of it was encompassed (compressed)
Though we didn't know that yet

Only that it was good to experience industry
And the taxonomy of systems & godheads
And already its breakdown

He walked on banks covered with wartystem ceanothus
Whose roots harbour nitrogen-fixing bacteria

The white flowers of high density
On his scented skin

Internal combustion engines drum in vessels
And pearls beyond absolute value, & pathogens

2

On the bus she
Experienced intercourse

Put a glove on her head the fingers sticking up
Shouted cock a doodle do

3

The stars fell down
Sang Bye Bye Blackbird

On the banks of the Guadalquivir
With the ratchet in his waist

Gulls scream over the water
On the errant alto sax, the player at the harbour

Big glass, simulacra
Fake junk, lazy arpeggios

Swans & cormorants
On the tern raft

Jellyfish at sea
Below the stars of the main sequence

He names them: Betelgeuse, Fomalhaut,
Mollusc, Alcor, Princess of Ethiopia,
Radar (Rede), Ulum, Dread

The family at war, at table
On the beach

Watch one star move
It's the American satellite, Johnny Too Bad

Collecting the heat
Of all the information yet to come

Chaconne

1995–96

for Trane
(49 variations)

After the rain
lost
in chrome dioxide
sound no more
words

Heard where the air filled
under the orange trees
the last sounds
so passed the hours
in the east

That you were part
of that
a spiral
organisation
gathered about waters

Blood & muscle
sound no more
the receiving station
lost
black bird phosphorescence

Dark
Ziryab would only sing
of that
framed
beauty

Invented a plectrum
of an eagle's wing
his power & method
spread through the Maghreb
in sound

The slave singer
tuned
roots
lutes
outshone poets

Sweet Qalam
was
a Basque girl sent when
young to study in the
east

Silk in her own tongue
legato & strophic
como rayo de sol
lost
the pain

Returned upon itself
a spiral
in the quantum void
riff
blood & muscle

Down
slowly behind the
shadow falls
off
it evaporates

Phosphorescence takes the
focus off
sensation of
hearing wood
in a forest

Maybe
a Miles groove
maybe collapsed lungs
the human experience
of burning nights

Instruments
fretted accordingly
spread
rosary of sound in
praise

A night with Bird the way
you blow
say
there was
logic in harmony

Rosary of sound
cut into the strophes
a durable epic
seldom
in the glamour

Play
lute
riff
preserve the link
allow grace

Words
because we are not
under the orange trees
sound
hieratic roots

Say there was logic in
harmony and you were
part
of that
engineered resonance

Hearing the
collapse of language
in
muscle & blood
riff

Say you were lost in
the Muslim
world
glory tumbled like
flutes so thickly gyric

Human moods
in a motley
art of words
in harmony
control

Broken verse
sung by everyone
played at prayer-time on
twenty-seven
drums of gold

The shadow falls slowly
down
behind phosphorescence
falls
gathered about waters

In the
dream
palace
of Al-Mahdi a hun-
dred *laúds* performed

Avempace would run
after the drover
so as
not to lose the
sound

Framed
in
the shell the blood
equinox
dreams

Speaks of patterning
in the Mozarabic
lute
jayal carrizo
laúd rota rabel

Black bird added a fifth
bird
black pearls
Africa lazy bird
shakes for grace

In different modes
play
xocra nura
play
dulzama gaita

Melodic
chain
in a single line
two simple canons paired
in spiral

Rustic rhythms
seven groups
in threes & fours
control
in the east

Trumpets straight & curved
shawms or *chirimías*
horn castanets
of burning
stones which crack in the heat

Words
overheard in the street
pitch
as if out of nowhere
pristine

Strange
oxides
filling the burning lungs
streams cut in the rock
rosaries of water

From Central Park West
amour
from Dahomey
fall
flutes

Dance
evaporates
the shadow
falls
in strange particles

The chords begin to flow
sweet
pastorale of ghosts
if you look hard enough
you'll see after the rain

Dreams
and schemes
on late night radio
allow grace
at the sharp moment

Sound
chases the train
heat
under the orange
grove *habib*

Praise
María Pérez
La Balteira plucked the
young soldiers
confessed to them

Africa
Alabama
speaks of
patterning
dance just for the love

Play the blues to Bechet
blues to Elvin
blues to you
desire the songs the slave
scales

On far-off summer nights
while
the melody of talk
stills you're
out

Your art
in the gold fluent tongue
organisation
broken mathematics
upward from the bass

You'll see
a love supreme
burst
free
air

The resonance
derived from
speed
angelic phrase-ends
cut into the strophe

Cut
fade sound & vision
when there is no longer
any sound the room is
filled

Allow
grace at the sharp moment
hieratic
"your sound has no more
words"

Red: Narrative Poem

1998–99

hello i.m. Kathy Acker

Chapter One: The Red Car

Find this red car

Find
this
red
car

If you find it, ring this number
It could be parked
on a double yellow
somewhere

Hope is running out
She is running out with pectorals blazing
We all remember her

How she's arching her eyebrows
which she had done orange
lying across the laps of the meanest looking muscle boys
in the back row
with wool caps huge radios glass pipes

In the absence of any
shred
there was no
no hope of
of looping back to
The boy died and then his mother died
The boy died and then his mother died
of grief?

Maybe

And a scientist or a doctor or poet could try to make sense of mere
sequence as an attempt at more reliable (or something) cognition

I'd like to do better than this
Meeting insults and violence
with trembling disdain
You put the boot in you put the boot in
You raises key questions
You was just a jerk-off
Just a jerk-off

He moaned and he nodded his long white bones dangled
Stuck in the clubhouse I seen blonde
I seen blonde I seen red
a muscular V6 engine
with advance 5-speed transmission
unique interactive 4-wheel drive
and sophisticated cruise control
eternal combustion mellowing 3 graces
all gone in 2 strokes till we're back
to 1 to 1 the brute facility
of making meaning of what may or may not have
the physicality of signs
where before there was nothing

All the seats ripped, all the skin broke
linguistically damaged
we have re-ordered
please credit

Is the price right

(Price includes delivery to dealer VAT 12 months road fund licence and vehicle registration fee and is correct at time of going to press, finance offer subject to status this offer cannot be used in conjunction with any other offer offer ends)

Chapter Two: Plage Mess

She said:

I'm in the middle of dirt
Inside the colours is a house
Water surrounds the house
I am starting from nothing. So slowly
I once said "a rose is my cunt"
I'm searching desperately for an airport
"there's no smoke without fire"
The street that I'm on is about to end
It was in this manner that I escaped being judged
Red's the colour of nerves when there is green
Who put dirt into each other's mouths and take the same out
with their lips
This is the beginning of the red room

Chapter Three: Awaiting Branding

Find this red car
    Get the number
Then it burst through
    Through the roadblock
With a half moon
    For a house guest
With a bad back
    When a job's done
On a dark floor
    Starting from nothing and
    searching for smoke and
    bleeding into the space
    of dirt
In a stagger of's body
    In a glint of a person
In the logics of bones
    Give you this
In a late swing
    In a big mess
In the absence of
    It's a tough ask
    as it might be
    having no skin
Having no skin
    Awaiting branding
Awaiting information
    Could it be read
Come from nowhere
    From a blank sheet
Awaiting judgement
    who he?
When freedom revolts
    and wants to name itself
    free trade
    free knives

starvation
feel good about your life!
These are the crunch days and
these are the crunch days
So far so good so far so good
so far so good and
These are the dark days and
these are the dark days
So far so good so far so good
who built this cage around them
These are the crunch days and
these are the crunch days
who built this cage around them
No messing!
Off the blade

Songs of the Permanent Way

2000

Sutton

Dirigible fruits
legged it over from
platform 4,
went into a fatal sulk
of blur & yellow.
Error = 02.
Doors whistle,
plain armies
funnel, strapped for
sauce. The ligatures
stand athwart
the buildings, striped
in light, and minimise
shearing forces
with a corresponding
reduction in
macular holes,
level or 90.
FEAR in black
on blue.

West Sutton

Station to station
a war-zone,
you'd think they
weren't or you wouldn't
think they were
used every day,
now lush and quite
horrible,
flutes, tyres,
broken mirror and
fucked wood
pigeon.

Sutton Common

An eight-car formation
towards the end of
the morning peak
cut with a down train
alive with sustenance
and comfort,
the former company initials
still proudly displayed
on the canopy.
Logos shine on what
superficially appears
to be open countryside
but the factories
are never far.
The wall of death
is steeply graded.

St Helier

Fox runs to nuzzle
garages, onion streak,
a collapsed pole,
a chair on the board
or shall my sword?
Leave without sound,
hush,
hieroglyph your
wall with lost
traces in the
raised part.
Soft columbines
mood the plaits,
customers reflect
in woodland.

Morden South

Go with the morning
spaces between habitats,
weeds grown over sleepers,
a joyous breadth.

Go with the flash
go sucking,
bricks do not make
a garage—
gather foxes & poppies.

Chiefly towards what
may migrate
an island platform
for reveries of
the future in liquid,
lighten a day
in surveillance.

South Merton

In the gardens
of our neighbours
skin is soft
with surface bloom,
shin bark.
Person to person
haunts the loping groove,
imagines flesh
with pride.

The signal is
fox, go
glove the aperture,
it is in the approach
and not

Wimbledon Chase

Distance moves but
foreground shifts
more swiftly
and so is accomplished
due time. Neurons
die and field loss
occurs. The looping
groves are flowing now.
Voices begin,
from the centre
from left and right,
arguing the toss
of a bright ball
of consequence.

Youths contemplate,
virgins arrive,
England
looking ragged.

Photons & icons
spangle the page
or is it
their dancing absences?

Wimbledon

It was something to do
with a crown
one time—a king,
the telephone
sales dept.
British electric lamps
on the permanent way,
extraneous but dull.
Beauty departs for home
as lipids cleave
to short-chain fatty acids—
we shall not see
their like again
until the next one
comes.
Sold—more wanted—
highlit
in acid yellow

Haydons Road

Summer in the
city—hot damn.
Don't
alight here,
domain of the
wasted conservatory,
domain of
sleepers
buckled life,
potter & float
in time
out of time
between
habitats.

Tooting

(hexagram 52)

The signal is
double yellow.
Extreme caution.
Keeping his back
perfectly still,
he loses all consciousness
of his body.

Horses.
Poppies.
The *in vivo* temperature
is 76°F. He walks
in the courtyard but
does not notice
those who linger.

A wave form
causes rucking up
on one side
of the insertion.

It kissed the top.
There will be no error.

Streatham

Dirt or dearth,
a colour gradient
hauled in down
time. Lips standing
proud of early.

Asleep in the grass,
your lot,
public address
feels sick.

All signs of life
missing.

Tulse Hill

Therefrom,
the curve of track
modulates
hope or moderates
rope, tensile with
its own going
until ways converge.
Ontological
flowers. Spate.
Garbage.
Do not touch the
live rail.

North Dulwich

(an invocation to the wild animals of the permanent way)

Gentle creatures
turn
from us! Give no
lip, not even
approximately.
Kindly go
or be
subsumed.
May sun beat
on fur or
flesh. Sing, steel,
for rust
shall clasp.

East Dulwich

Cheap perfume or
evidence of the ice age?

Cinders or paper
roses?

An alien ball
from another court?

Peckham Rye

Rust is first
and last and
kissed your
eye

Woodland enfolding
sweet chlorophyll or
rubber quite
smashes your
face with its
speed.
Angels in a bulkhead.
And the trees open,
songsters brood,
the apple goes
sour.

The Glory Boxes

2000–02

Glory Box: 1

when meadow reflections from the earth
moved swiftly celestial keeping light
on the threshold of form
the bedroom unlocked as a dream.
By night or day across the desert things
broadly divided into two
categories
the tree itself or its
process of fruit-bearing
when the heavens had lifted a little
while the birds turned
headlong, into a
cauldron of figures,
recklessly mixing
to a field, to a tessitura
of time
to reach the end of the
unpredictable periplus.
And while a thought dissipated
in terms of its
deductions and
consequences for the
future
and with the heart covered with hair
the series led into
fundamental errors of
conception.
While worlds written by evolution call on every side
while signal coloration shines, and leaps
from existing objects, to
ensembles of probable
objects
to groups of differing
objects
spinning in a new direction, trailing
diverse material

the light is on his way
towards true continuity,
this being
to see-saw from one to
the other.
And even with something focused on the wall behind
some fragments from blackness under eyelids shaped
as if with fractured smoke
give rise to striking
contrasts, due to
accompanying semblance. Haunted when in water
to go beyond tempered
space
let me hear those drifting coronal lesions

Glory Box: 2

cyan flow
fractal & pure.
How to
start? Emotional
glamorous show, or
technical
(constraints)
sound quality
notes, listen
to other &
imagine (but don't
hear anything
yet).
Put file
add all
done, tell
the emotion
in one
glow at the
early
horizon.
Begin with
fragments, a
problem
solving
exercise, doodle
white
with purpose
unrelated &
physical improv-
isation
linked
along the
shoreline.
I have
started off

with the most empty
formulae; the
distinctive parts
these lines
marmorialised
since childhood,
developed later,
are you
saying
I'm not
allowed to
break syntax?
The worst
is often the
beginning, does
emotion really
start things
off? Lots of
music doesn't
have much emotional
content.
And the
architecture
of
the world
is laid
before us,
made a
compromise
with
differential
equations. To
go
from emotion
into art, think
technically,
surprise.
I cannot
but reflect

on
grace, the
chances are
starting to
recede,
        change
        the past
        for music
        is a social art,
not often
do I call
your
memory
into
question.
Trade up
                have more
                freedom of
                experimentation,
                as he
                put it, we forget
a bit go
chilly
quite
serious
your
knees will
shake
                momentarily
                about the
                astronomical
                origin of the
                problem.
        Composers
        in the past
had to
dine on
swallows
in syrup,

you may copy
out music, they
learned by
copying. What is
the right duration?
Stellar
orbits in
galaxies, on a
time scale of
some 200
million
years, take
on a threedimensional
character –
I would
take fresh
country
milk
above all
other, or
maybe
just a
thought.
The point
of a starting
point is to
move away
from it.
So there was
no drama.
Invention &
detachment, name
the things you
like,
instead of
making perfect
ellipses.
You can make it
out of anything,

it's what
you do with it.
Impose
pitches on a pattern
as difficult to
visualise
in a
rotational way,
when the
orbits are
real as when
they are
used by
mediaeval &
eastern musics
(as above) but
imaginary
constructions in
phase space.
The rooks
click on,
always the same
interval
or rotating
intervals, make
anchor at
star & not
in utter
nakedness,
a page of material,
everything
is in the
detail.
Then compose
with that.
Life in the
festival
of coronal
bliss

appears to have
always
involved
a continuous
struggle
for survival.
I find the
fugue
at heart too
much to
invent, & submit
to chance
within a particular
organism's
environmental
niche.
Then be ruthless
bear & laugh
at the
darling
pygmy
chords!
kick around
& not not fall
in love
too soon.
Repetition is good
because you don't
hear the second
time in the same
way.
In effect,
the sensory
mechanics of
an organism
teach the
rules of the
game,

require specific
segments to be
functionally
altered in response
to changes
to members
of the
cast before
moving them
in the
environment.
Typically, orbits
would wind their
ever more
complicated paths
around, cf a barber's
timepiece in three
dimensions or
more, creating a
dark scribble
in space with
sections
repeating material
at these
lengths. (The
internal
structure that
could not be seen
from the
outside.)
Load into
browser,
toggle volumes,
set at cyan
20%, black
100, I love
the group
difference between
speeds of

composing
& listening,
at your
disposal.
The earth's
gravitational
field has been
continuously present,
it is this
isomorphism
that we
can imagine.
The 2 poles
of insistence
here could be
establish
stuff &
change it.
I bear in mind
(a) hermetic
selfsufficiency,
or
(b) the journey
towards
total
explication,
as where
experiences
over the
entire duration
of red &
green
are inverted but
the needs of the
country, the
needs of my
people, and
all structural
properties

of life on earth
remain
the same.
One who is
loved
plays
the piano
in an adjacent
room,
it is for
their
welfare that I
choose my
projects. But with
complicated strange
attractors, projection
just smears
the detail
into an indecipherable
mess.
The success
of our adaptation
to earth's +1G
gravitational
environment serves
to emphasise
words,
make them longer,
change pitch (up?
down?), louder,
leave pause
before or after,
to make such an
evolutionary
transition
almost trivial.
Think about
your text before you
throw music
at it!

Those
properties will
be directly
represented
in the
structure
of [my]
awareness,
                    discontinuity,
                   bursts of noise,
                   Cantor dusts –
Write down the
            hierarchy, do
            graph of intonation
            & work out where
            the pauses are
(the domain
name I was
before I
was born),
            then work slowly into
            the music speech.
A thump
of bombs
in the
hills
changes the
air pressure
in the
room,
                    phenomena
                      like these
                    had no place
                        in the
                     geometries
                     of the past.
            A rhythm
            based
diction

of sincerity
among strangers
        is one
        end of the
        continuum
        (recitative) –
        song is the
        other, where trailing
                    cloud
moving two
thousand years
across
the country
from the
east
blurs the
categories,
        the melody takes
        over, tension
floods boom
        (*aria*) between
        "pool of motifs"
        and speech
        rhythm,
as food
blooms
        or vocal
        line takes
        off into
        a melody from
        sprech-
        gesang.
                As far
                as the
                system is
                concerned,
            nothing unusual
            has happened,
        the

edge feels more
like an ongoing
opera than a
number one, reducing
room for the
thought,
"Hmm!
Something
strange
just happened!"
to words, repeating
small fragments
of
text. Sometimes
you don't
need the words –
If
there were to be
such a thought
it must float
entirely free
in the house,
the music
could make the
point, or tell
the story. Harmony
in the
house of love.
The system
can vary
it by using predominance
of notes, using tonics
& dominants
(contrasting
areas). Heterophony
not quite the
same as unison
blurring next
time in time

and
utterly
impotent
to affect
later
processing

of all
human
beings.
Intimacy is
concerned with
space
& objects.
When I see you it is as though
this event has a different location
perhaps early evening, a little way down
the park the winter moon over
Roberts Capsule Stopper Co Ltd.
The remembered call of the song-thrush.
And yet
it is reported
that in parts
of the colour spectrum
there is
no ebb
& flow
between such
remarkable functions
as complex adaptive
behaviour & reproduction.
No
need for
friends to
think alike. Un-
fortunately there are systematic
reasons why these methods
must fail. When I see
You, whose physical processes will not go on for ever
a low rumble (flows) occurs
in a red car the winter stumps
the engine
out of which

a purpose
grows
it is reported, vital processes a "raw"
sensation in the park, entailed by duration
and measurable quantities. Peak
intensity is associated with *knowing*
how to unconscious, synchronised
to the upper level cluster.
For example,
Messiaen's transcriptions of birdsong.
I see you, I note your loved limbic cortex & the way emotions
are associated with this, my fair guide
at the keyboard in numbered
shirt. All this
was a
transitional
phase in the
history
of relations.
You are so transient, I weep to connect, yet vehicles pass
in the street below unconcerned
the orange against the black
so effective in low-grain, high-contrast
presentation, as verb becomes noun
heavens above, forget it.
My energy
is failing,
my mind
is set, the side
effects are minimal. A temporal door
opens we pass through it but with
little risk, for we live here quite easily
You at your keyboard I at mine, replacing
parts of speech, emerging selves
gathered up anew into coherences
that save us from false cognates &
bad monologues, though even now
I fear I have walked into a wave.
When I see you – but I don't, for

you are in the next room, all I do
hear is the evidence, the maybe
chords, the gilded edges
transformed
thereof, that convince me, inasmuch
as I can be, that life occurs,
elsewhere, on the planet that turns
into the dark and, at some point
on the graph, out of it and back –
certain processes are taking place,
at the level of neurons & molecules
(the chords recurring) so that the neural
circuits are etched with this fact,
the fact of you that I intuit, and the awe that occurs,
in my mind, that I possess, my
curiosity
is manifest. But do I own my mind?
Or am I in it? my right mind, I mean,
whose continuity is assigned to me.
Is *this* a bad monologue?
Then men
& women
must
despair.
I hope
not. A wave, of sorts.
You who require a careful theoretical analysis
freeze the works!
that I may first stare at stars in the
darkling. Or forget it. I am not easily
memoried, especially not, not at
keyboard, not with people like us.
"My life
will start
only
when I stop
this
masquerade."
When you find you have something

then what you have got is nothing
but the fear of its fading, don't you find?
No, this is no prerequisite it's a ruffle
it is quite vertiginous to come saucy
and misharmoniously plunge
in the air no more than a quake of
attention a light & diaphanous
unknown, to alter the parameters
by no means, a point or cyclic
attractor a transient subtree lost
video data in the snow of the
Russian tundra on a screen near you.
You who long to be elsewhere in another time another place
I start
with the
present and
work back
to this
conclusion, giddy shots of "movie-
in-the-brain" that start to break
up the control gibberish of might
have been, such as perception
of the colour red
shifts in attention
thresholds mapping the unknown
regions pertaining to such entities
As if you could. As if anyone.
"The mind will survive explanation,
just as a rose's perfume,
its molecular structure deduced,
will still smell as sweet." As if
"We never
speak about
ourselves."
Smouldering, the embers fell
back and a feeling of ease dispersed
among the participants. Sunshine
over the M11. A jay flew suddenly
out of the Rye. The sea at Hunstanton,

and people in it. To whom
is (was) this happening? The very hours
leave us, one by one, removing
themselves from our considered
presence. And so much that this entails.
When the digits turn over will that change
be manifest in the rapid movement of a bird
a small impulse that
did
not move
mountains
within a larger one that turns without
being owned? I lost it somewhere,
I think, that base I started out from,
Bach on the radio, I thought it was you, for every moment
that turns away from us leaves us
equally bereft, we will never
see its like again.
In the vast
emptiness
my apologies. A quarter-note, a chord, drops
into the air and falls clean out of it
leaving only its memory clinging
to the next, and then that in turn dropping
away into the great mystery
that is the past.
Your voice in it, its physical structure something
precious that I fear may be down-
graded or vanish entirely, I want
to rush & cherish it but by now
it may no longer be there & my aim
already's thwarted in its ways,
my eloquence
is gone,
I am
growing
obsessive, and
despair

Glory Box: 4

feeling the
coolness
of the
descending
melodic pattern
under my hand
at bars 1–11
listening,
I struggle, brighten
after a bad start.
At bar 7 a Great
Tit comes to
feed
much munching for bodily homeostasis.
No progress
(little progress),
and perceiving
the trees
reflecting
through the
window
glory crashes.
At bar 8
a mistake.
My life
is constantly
thrown headlong
oh, the dark mornings,
the dark parts of the spirit.
Bars 1–11 are
repeated;
uncannily aerobical,
into transcendent
purchase,
Blue Tit comes
to feed

rampaging solid
into the wee
things, and passes
during
the fourth
repetition
wholly
outside me.
If we imagine
a Great Tit
comes to
feed, bar 17,
a space in itself
with which the
perceiving subject
(persuaded with
great
difficulty)
contrives to
coincide,
if I imagine
a lighter case,
if I am thinking this I am no longer having the experience that led to the thought
Bars
17–24 at a slower
tempo:
the Magpie,
bright as she was
with some needles and
her new German boyfriend.
Uniformly high,
my hand
perceives the
distance
between
bars 17–24
as it spans,
becomes able
to know,

devising & rehearsing…
but people started getting nervous.
If it be insisted
that the
sensation
intermittent, incoherent,
having no fixed sequence
of ideas, rambles,
built out of breakages
and if I am writing this I am no longer having the thought
in my thumb
of something that
didn't work.
At bar 18 a Blue
Tit comes to
feed.
Some inconclusive material hands
are shown on a video screen
tippexing out texts
and in my
first finger
are at any rate
"signs" of the
distance,
"Nothing ever becomes
still enough
for us to hold."
At bar 20, song
of the Blackbird
in early
spring,
how could
these processes of stripping
and building
come to have
in themselves
any means of
signifying
links

and if I am are reading it I am once removed from having written
to leave the line edges ragged
and let them grate
to get beautiful discords.
Error at bar 21.
Self-heckled
method & technique,
negative & positive power
blur into complex knots,
relationship
between points
in space,
bars 17–24 are
repeated,
unless they were
already
slightly faster.
At the repeat of
bar 21, a Great Tit,
"always at the same distance
from the substance",
is scared away
by sudden
noise noise
even within a wall of noise.
Light
thresholds of social polyglossia
verticalised stripes of dark matter
are they by force or decree
situated on a
path running
from one
to the other?
by faculty or image a
silence without codes?
A thought
is by degree or skill
really
transcended

by its
objects
and if I am listening to the writing read back I am in a different space already
a skin of noise
palimpsest of anecdote,
with a hint of.
Bar 24, aircraft
sound.
Crows in the
distance,
the paradoxes in ethnic cleansing
within fractal forms.
No birds sang.
The first snows of the winter
would find them
proliferating
and if I am reflecting on what I have heard I am in a further space of memory
Bars 30–42, crushed
chords, the
tempo appears
to have
changed
simultaneously interest rates
are plummeting.
Dusk.
High-realist, micro-detailed,
panoramic photos,
their relation-
ships to each
other, then
it was time to go
to stave off the hunger.
At bar 32, a
mistake,
finding its
way through
turning upside down
in the study and then
tried to have another go.

It is I who
reconstitute
the historical
and if I am thinking about the memory my thought has begun to take a different shape
I who recognise
in it
at bar 33, a
mistake.
Welding and blowtorching,
I begin
reordering the
groin in springlike sunshine
and I should
have no thought
happily on the bus.
At bar 40 a Blue
Tit comes
to feed,
get rid of all the fruitiness,
get rid of the beauty
of it,
it's not beautiful at all.
Some of it is.
Doesn't hold water this
does it
but it wouldn't make sense as a piece
had I
not within
myself all
that is needed
to invent it.
Great difficulty.
The hands
come out of
alignment,
clocks dragged
and we carry with caution
the responsibility,

it is I
who assign
to my thought
thus trammelled
the objective
of resuming
the action,
the piece now
racing towards
a hiatus
and I who
with triplets in the left hand
verify my
thought's
orientation
its profiles
of behaviour
soon
established
towards this
objective
but it's in the balance of things,
so what can I say.
Unless thought
itself had put
into things
what it
subsequently
finds in them,
and it has become a different thought I am thinking
it would have
no hold
upon things,
the questions
answered
by provision
and would be
an "illusion
of thought"

the metronome
marking
fixed
in light

Glory Box: 4, i.m. Alaric Sumner

Glory Box: 5

would set
limits
to this one
world
where
at any
instant
the fields of sleep
are strong:
if
you could
move in
one
direction
only if
great tits & blue
tits came
in guise of
mistakes
illusions and
questions
to your hand
to be fed,
one by
one
loved or
not loved
or only
partly then
I should like
to believe
I live
in this
or this, or
some other
one

world –
let me hear
a thought of
birds thus sing-
ing they
are indeed
mistakes
illusions
and questions
and lovely is
their trumpets,
one becomes
one, & one
is two
and two
are loved
and lovely,
become
none other
than
one
for sorrow
two for
joy
in process of
making
mistakes
and all the earth
turns past
conscious-
ness of mis-
laying
two and
takes
two,
treecreepers
nuthatches
and adds a
third.

Once
there was a time
you would
only see
such wood-
land birds
rarely
in the city
to
give one
piece of
data
of a
particular
such that
& even
so
& even pied
woodpeckers
would show
mistakes
to be the origin
which is
revealed
through glory
so one
appears
in part-
icle flux
and then an-
nihilates
immediately
and then an-
other
one that
can sometimes
be heard.
It is not now
come to me from
a unity distinct

the word
could be
thus
identified
as an instrument
of action
remained a
third person
process
gratuitous, a
phenomenon
of thought
other
than
tawny
owls sadly,
apparelled in
waters
describe
a disturbance
of thinking
they come
and go,
come
and go, the
one and then
the next, the
third,
and more,
once they are
recognised
every common sight
comes and goes
and there
remains a
difference:
birds have
vanished
for
contingency

is not a
break in
stuff
nor is a
problem
given
that thought
a timely utterance,
to be
solved
at any time
upon the
waters
within the
contingency
of the
world.
And the
forms of
presence
a small
colony of
nesting
jackdaws
survived &
are necessary
consequences
of zero
dimensions
or one,
two, three
or more
by night or day, the
freshness of a dream
rising by one
and two and
three or
more,
not-
with standing

(added a
fourth)
in the south-
west corner
they gather
their devices,
jays stripping
acorns from twigs
the blue ghost
of a bicycle
on the stair,
the paper
and the trees.
They sound their
warning
a few
feet above
your head
the moon,
the earth
which moves
all things
away into
distance,
the land and sea
which
is thought
loaded with
sediment
now
trimmed to
transparency,
they flash
into cover
in ones &
twos &
compound
groups
from
celestial light,

echoes
virtually
disappeared
at the slightest
sign:
sparrows,
feral pigeons
where
I place my
feet
they must
lay hold
of something –
thrushes &
starlings
throng the winds
and when
he cannot
anchor him-
self he is ill
at ease,
even
on the wide
surface,
and fidgets
and hops
this way and
that,
where
the heavens are bare
round me,
have taken up
residence,
flutters
or flies
off and comes
down
to sound
no more
the things which

Glory Box: 6

stuff
happened
to become
the memory
of past
events:
tea with the
family,
much munching
with light
upon them
obliterated,
and yet
there was
distant howling
of persons,
or of foxes
in the urban
environment –
such a
state,
could be
a wedding
or a festival,
not far
removed –
wherefore
he frames
his song,
appalled
at the malign
network,
pausing to
sonically trace
its contours –
takes tired,
dehydrated limbs

to the box
and finds
the men
decorative and
ingratiating,
but she by contrast
impresses,
being impossible
in colour,
and so he,
in the midst
of changing
his socks,
immediately
launches
into a
confused tale
of having been
found wandering
and told
to stay in
a strange room:
you must
admit that
the previous
business, love
or strife
or whatever, has
by now
perished
and that
the present
is a
new exterior
place of
thought that
broods like
the trees
on which

those birds
do rest –
furthermore,
if the living
power of
the mind
is imported
into our
already
completed bodies
at the moment
when we are
plunged into
the first page
crossing the
threshold
of life,
one would
not then
expect to see
it grow
with the body
and the limbs
in the very
blood; rather
one would
expect it
to live
in total
isolation,
as in
a cage of
blond wood
and chrome,
while still
managing to
flood the whole
body with
sensibility

flecked with
beige spume –
and yet
the existence
of this intimate
connexion
is a patent
fact; solemn
but absolutely
perfect
blood lovely
too-seriously
stuff,
interpenetration
of the body
through the veins,
flesh, sinews,
and bones,
sweatily rotten
at the top
and side
where flood
has damaged it
(what larks)
so even
the teeth
are given
a share
in sensation,
caused by
icy water,
salade niçoise
and a blond
beer
or the crunching
of rough grit
concealed
in a piece
of bread –

cool, grey-
blue
endings, then,
are nothing
to us
and do not
affect us
in the least,
now that the
nature of
such space
is understood
and as
in times past
when the
pipes were
making an ugly
rhythmical noise
we felt
no distress,
when the
whole earth
shudderingly
quaked
with fabulously
beautiful vocal writing
beneath the
coasts of
high heaven,
when
thunder approached,
with such
whistles & flashes,
rain began
to lash, and
the kebab, too,
was rapidly
cooling,
we continued,
it wasn't

different
in this
way, when we
are no more,
when a
strangely quiet
sun declines, and
body
and soul,
upon whose
union
our being
felt fixable,
are divorced,
when the
bulldozers
have moved
into the
Rye, perhaps
displacing
the foxes
that perhaps
lived there,
and screeched
with love
in spring past,
you may
be sure
that nothing
at all
will have
the power
to affect us
or awaken
sensation
in us, who
shall not
then as
particulars exist –

as a man
who had
fallen, and struck
his head
on paving,
quite still
and bluish,
a red stain
on the ground
round his head
and a small
smear to mouth
while a crowd
stood, not without
struggle, not even
if the earth
be commingled
with the sea,
both physically
and psychologically
and the sea
with the sky
reconfigured
the bed-
room would one
recall this one;
this who was
one, and lies
profoundly still
and very small
as though
a vast
distance away,
and yet
you felt
you could
wake him
by calling
and it spits
with cool

rain from time
to time,
but those
dark ones
that shine shall not
be seen
again
for between
that life
and this
lies an
unbridged gap –
everything
radiantly
present
(or absent):
an interval
during which
all the motions
of our atoms
strayed and
scattered
in all directions,
nudging the edge
of mistakes
with confidence
assembling and
redistributing –
far away
from sensation,
when those who
remain take
a walk
in the woods,
looking back
through the
bygone ages
that elapsed
before
our birth

and yet
were nothing
to us –
here, then,
is a mirror
in which nature
shows us
the time
to come
even for a few
minutes
the time after
which is all
put by
and he who
ended his life
thus ditching
under a blue
scuddy-cloud
sky with
today's light
on the
disconnected
tubes
will remain
no less long
in the after-
math
than one
who perished
many months
and years ago –
and so
with changeable
weather: clouds
periodically
drifting across,
temperature
veering sharply,

we drive, the
silver light
    of the sun
    aslant of us
    into the dusk –
    and yet

Glory Box: 6, i.m. Charles Francis Edwards (1915–2000)
and Douglas Oliver (1937–2000)

"There's something in there..."

2003

for John Tilbury

There's something in there.

At least … there may be. Who can say more than that?

It comes in there, or *is* there, sometimes. It's suggestive of...

No-one can say what it is.

What?

What is out here is found. It was found in the woods. In the dark woods, in the midst of it all. Like the poet, in the midst of a journey, it steals away.

It's out here. It's made of steel.
Steel in the woods. It curves, all the way in.
A steel cave, and what's in it.

There's definitely something in there.

But one can never be definite.

Let's say a probability.

A throat. There are rivets all down its throat. But that's not it. What it is, is in there, as opposed to out here. By out here is meant all that isn't in there. But where would *there* be?

It's a throat, and a gnarl in the throat. Something gnarled.
Like in the woods, a gnarling, throat rivets. Or a tongue.

That would be something.

There are rivets all the way down the tongue of the thing, if it is a thing, and not just a space.

You see, it could be infinitely deep. The spaces could be silences. They could phosphoresce, that is, liquefy.

Where does this thought happen?

There are some things here you don't even *want* to think of. You can't, you can't say the words properly. They used to say it was because you had a short tongue. A poet would understand, sometimes the space seems infinitely deep, and at other times it's like a patch of dark velvet affixed to the outside. *I* comes in there, *I* subsequently speech-compensate for this, as though the lake of my heart, as the poet says, almost destroyed…

What?

The poet would understand.

I mean that it's in there, not the rivets, the rivets go all the way down to it, or you go down. Say it's a part of your brain. Or your mouth.

Inside your mouth.
Where the harmonic series dances.

Or *my* mouth, if you like. *In* my mouth. Or on my tongue.

I know that!

"This heart within me I can feel, and I judge that it exists. This world I can touch, and I likewise judge that it exists."

It is said a poet said that.
He said it in the woods.
No-one knows any more.

It could be that someone was lost.

Lost in the woods. Or lost in thought. It's the same thing.

By that is meant, that one kind of space is replaced by another kind. You go from the outside to the inside, it can't be explained any further than that. You'll have to look it up. You go from out here to in there, meaning…

There may not be any in there.

What was that?

I can't say. It's private. Never mind. *I* am privileged to do so. You what? *I* do have access to it. Or … it depends.

I can hear a voice.

It moves from in there to out here, and then back again. If you get the drift. It is reminiscent of foxes in the garden, just before dawn. The little foxes with big ears. You need a keen ear. Like the little dog, you know, the little dog peering down that great trumpet, in the old wind-up days, but who can say if a sound emanates, and if it emanates what it signifies, and if it signifies, what does *that* signify? For instance, is it significant? To the dog, that is. A little dog, white with brown spots. Let's call him Spot. "I am I because my little dog knows me." A poet said that. Is the dog even looking for significance, or authority, say? The question is, who is to be the master?

But it could be comforting. It could be the only comfort he has, this evidence of private space, emanating into public space, replacing replacing replacing…

Well, there's a certain pleasing symmetry about that, dog on one end of the trumpet, god on the other. Symmetry can substitute for certainty.

Where was I?

I could say that I believe there is something in there.
Although I have no grounds for such a belief.

The dog Spot got up and walked away. He walked away from his master and god.

eight + six

2003

Mostly for Elaine

PART I

Darkly Slow*

Bring back the persons! I
Ups & says
                                they are bipolar & splendid
The jogger in the park, the murderer in the dark
They're so lonely, they speculate, give em something to do
The imaginary persons right here
Wherever that may be, beloved, awed
And in a cloud (a crowd)
                                                    he she & you
Catching the eye, ordering a round for the unknowables

Bring em all back, I don't want to see them go
One's at a university in the snow
Another on the beach, one praying for the souls in woe
Oh sad poet please be on your toes
The boat casts off, the buddleia grows
And what's behind the moment's horizon no-one knows

** The title is a direct translation of Elliott Carter's "Adagio Tenebroso".*

The Anthropic Principle

This is not me (says Me)
a terpsichore of invention, it is what I
says or transforms to blaze or daze
as in the sun or certain main-sequence stars
which make the carbon of "my" culture
whither it becomes the social body
through ratio & constant* that could have been
no other number.
                                        And for our next
a jump-technology of reference
that changes, hazes
come down to us through the fm band
Oh the trombones bark
                    The forest is young again
                                        So fill me [____] in

* Planck's Constant (6.6262 x 10^{-34}) governs the nucleosynthetic process by which stars convert hydrogen to the heavier elements of which we are made.

Lambently Fluid

Is there a better way of saying this?
I hope so. Did the dog
beg her master for the stick
to be thrown? And did she give
unconditional love, obeisance, abasement?
Did summer come & go?
Were resources wasted? Did the park
turn from green to brown & back to green?
Do any here know what they are, can we ever know, these intangibles of comfort
their cheeks to our jowls, who sometimes stay with us for a while but eventually
get up & go, allowing others to join us in their turn, & still others after them
the spaces cumulating until finally they too take their leave & all is as before?

Lunar Holography

Did you see our shadow creep up on the moon* stealing a
bite of luminosity? That was Thursday—well
I write this in the interim or do I mean
the ante-room where it seems as though I'm slowly being
rotated under a bright light did you
ever get that feeling? When you are no longer there
each trip, a rare adventure in prospect
ends the same way, mildly toxic, no problem

Ghosts in the plumbing, fox rot in the suburban verge
beer & biriani would do it—or not, for I am
wrecked without you and would have you return forthwith.
I send packages into that ether men do call foreign
parts, hoping for reciprocity—what comes back:
the "Don't panic" code, smoke moving behind the lights

* Lunar eclipse visible in London, 9/10 December 1992.

The Engine of Love

Dark drizzle falls & falls the sparkling dark
rain falls as evening falls on the football pitch
on the Ex-Servicemen's Club & Social Centre
where bitter's a pound a pint & where talk too
is cheap on a Saturday night—as over the table
over the numbered balls a boy confronts
his Dad who grips the cue in his big fists—
the boy's eyes flash with anger
                                        at this moment
for the first time he drives the engine of love
but he's out of control—he pleads for its return—
beer spills on mica, video talk resumes
outside rain logs into the abandoned turf
great pylons march without a motion to
the power station on the distant coast

The Panic Museum
(Theory of Poetry)

Falling to pieces in this brilliant backwater
with 800 years of delusions washing around me
now I lose track of the evening session
as conversations disconnect behind me.

I'd spent too much time placing out the plastic chairs
I decided, for the audience that would never come:
folk from the ante-room, burning with rhetoric
the liquidated stock in the panic museum.

First among them being the pope of fright
absent as always, though here in his manor he
's passed the law to his clones to keep safe.

(Watched by drunk students, two swans drift in moonlight
asleep on the placid water their necks plunged through
their feathers (they did not change my life).)

To the Estuary

To the estuary's wooden hulks I travel
along the sandlings where animals cry again
bass lines of bombers again over
dance fields over the class system of old England.
It is essential the trappings are slowly stripped away
hydrochloric acid is useful for this or a blowtorch or
some dead good corrosive so that through the foggy air
I may again believe this was not what I saw:

A quantity of animal dung in the bottom of the boat
a lighted doorway again I am in
the summer house in autumn where shapes move
in unison or conflict we look in and on and over
through and from where the paint burns
a sheen into the soft-hard air in England's daylight

Above the Shining Roofs

I had the air about me   Fractured
Greyish in the sodium lamplight
in front of the Rye Hotel   Oh gentle pint!
Oh friend oh lifestyle choice!

Outward in a zigzag
from the Cambrian beach this once was
ambience plunged towards the zero degree
of the bathroom shelf

From a higher energy state in negative space
the lights had come on one by one
to make of monochrome those great

rich blacks   Above the shining roofs I swear
as god is my fax machine
hung tears or drops of golden blood

Trembling in the Berserk Station

Today came to life at 6.30 am, found him
trembling in the berserk station
where he remained until 6.50, then got up
in darkness to hunt for a shirt.

Out at 7.08 in remnants of freezing fog
first the newsagent's then onward still—
The fog hung heavily in hollows round tracks
as the train pulled out towards the light

Suppose you were trying to do something
impossible, like, from memory that isn't there—
Suppose … well then it wouldn't be healing so much

as being already well
or stepping out of the time track
in which the disease occurs.

Becoming

You see that to come into your own
is not an easily achievable wish
falling within its own allusive rubric
for you yourself are still the helpless baby
or a housecat scratching at upholstery
in the quite awful confines
of your history & ceremony
the source of all that stuff you hate so much.
But, luminous with wine, you watch
the one lying on the hospital bed & your image
mirrored, and slowly it becomes less hard:
the window is a source of light too, after all,
the architecture & the plan
become more clear: it's not you not you…

I Go to Sleep

I go to sleep in the railway buildings
which someone said looks like a boat
For five years I had that fine panorama
spread out before me until winter came with
sunny chill I wore my leather put it in a poem
I went to sleep & woke to oh just mountains
of phone messages & somehow after that
things were not quite the same
Look — I want
to put this & this & those
together so it has a thing inside the line
(the dark line that flits & jags)
which maybe is what I call poetry who can
say, which is no fugue & which is mine

The Coral Necklace*

Then we take the path on down the valley
accompanied perhaps by a hopeful dog
through all that tumbling fecundity of oak & alder
fir & pine, & eucalyptus, vetch, wild lilies
lemons ripening in their picture cage of netting
& in the bend before us the sea glistening hazy still the
Siren rocks amid it pink & purple white
so there we drink our water

Now I've opened the curtains this a.m.
& it's frozen upon the garden
a shade encroaching hard on fugitive glitter
How a year can go by, then another
it's in the earth somewhere, ochre & silver
sometimes your tongue can taste the coast

* *Sorrento and London, May 1993, and six months later…*

I Go to Sleep (2)

I go to sleep in the railway buildings
                                                            whereupon
a child appears, shining amid design specifications
says press space bar now
                                             I am a directory called stenosis
recalling mental sex as though the pointing device
had gone berserk all values had come out
as surplus value   But I remember being that child
discovering the sentence in the midst of speaking it
which was a very intelligent and a human thing

I go to sleep in England but where do I wake up?
for blood travels to my face and darkens my perception
into a sulcus of unwavering belief which is stupid stupid
I go to sleep as the fabric shivers
the aircraft shimmers the sentence dissolves
into the ultra-violet

Management Development

He comes & goes into & out of your
spectrum of issue avoidance, & that's cool
it's what you want & don't want in the opera
of your craving for the new
and no less than totally interesting, saying yes
you'd love to & meaning it, speaking of wanting to go
there with him as well but not wanting
to get too close, not great, but all we have

You clearly saw & it's ok it really is

You did like them & put them on

I had to say this sooner or later & in the end
as good as did though you'll agree "as good as"
isn't as good as
            so you could bat the charge right back to me
but didn't   & I love that in you too

Like

My love is like

Oh no it isn’t

And its loss is like

For heaven’s sake

Like, what if it were all a
big mistake?

Because you’re jealous & so
judgemental

You can’t talk to me like that
what can I say

Because you have some
personal opera going on

Its music, what, huge
like a locomotive
imaged at strange resolutions

No   Nothing like that

It’s too luminous a conceit?

It’s enough to change the
shape of a man’s head

It hurts like fuck
it hurts my, like, human heart
you know what I mean

I mean nothing is like anything else*

* *This line is stolen from Eric Mottram. Something always to bear in mind.*

American Music

When Jimmy Cobb hit that high cymbal*
when the metal went liquid & blue
all the cats in the farmyard woke from golden slumbers
in the twilight of money†
                                        Now
there ain't nobody here but us (white) chickens
beside the red wheelbarrow
Oh that doesn't work any more, this farm's not so funny
ripped & jammed up on which so much de-

pends like in the west it's always after the
war the junk belief jammed up the thing
his thing my thing our thing the changes
kind of hard edged pursuivant on strange information
Oh Jimmy Cobb oh Frank O'Hara we're waiting
for you, get up get it on
do the business—

* *Jimmy Cobb, drummer with the Miles Davis band, 1958–63. The cymbal shot referred to comes 1'30" into "So What" on* Kind of Blue, *right on Miles' entry; as everybody knows, this was the moment when the world went from monochrome into colour.*

† *"In the twilight of money" is a phrase attributed to Le Corbusier.*

Shipwrecked and Comatose

Euphoria I hear you calling
Euphoria begins to wash off
leaving a pale petulance at such roughage
that seeps between—no more—
this is a tradition I just invented
all for you. Excuse me have we finished
discussing this yet? You, a woman of my
own age? Or something?
So that now I feel the ennui of one who hasn't had much congress with
    real persons
Who is dull with sun & bluster on a charabanc trip to the seaside on
    Bank Holiday Monday
The faint hope lurking that distorts judgement Euphoria come back it's
ok I'll make a deal with you

Chamber Music*

You have a great wide window Chris through which
sunbeams flash, reverberate on four
white walls a dark stained floor—it's a good
window for a good & useful space
Now we're tuned up—but I just want to say
The Art of Fugue's not something to be hacked through
as one might chainsaw a viola in half
by some careless mischance (finding oneself
with the wrong implement for the occasion)
                                                                      Hey
what is this piece of wood doing in my hands?
where am I? You mean the city's turned &
summer's coming through?
                                                    Welcome to
Planet Earth—
home of Johann Sebastian Bach

* *For Chris Shurety, on his 50th birthday.*

Deliciously Fauve

Summer heat
envelops the flimsies
the thing you did, the number five
shooting straight, deliciously fauve
you wanted one of those, I wanted
to remake them all with my corrections
oh it's so sweet to be listing on the wing
just give the man a smoke he needs a boost that thing
wasn't right, I need coating with foil after
such a marathon, with brightness to
reflect the summer's heat and
keep from dehydration
under big glass & no
sense of time

They Didn't Go Home

The poets and their entourages, appendages,
readerships, theoretical props and absences
are variously and severally assembled.
A shows pictures and reads the words.
B takes seriously the notations in cowboy comic balloons.
C vacillates, and comes down on the side of externality.
D demonstrates conviviality (again).
E emphasises the smallness of the audience.
F is quiet and has with him a pair of roller blades.
G, as usual, enigmatic.
H waxes shaven.
I have had my hair newly cut but have forgotten about it.
Sound travels from the street below because it is a warm night & there is no reason for folks to go home.

The Poets Gather
(Theory of Poetry 2)

The poets gather. They, like poetry itself,
want to be, not seem. Which is seemly.
These are their stories, and the summation
of them is this: that they reject story.
Why, they are paralytic with joy: on their plastic chairs
they identify the depth of field of such paradoxes
and exult in it — they presuppose no need
for emotional closure.
That was then. And now?
Well, only you & I are left, and we're engaged
in refutation. Yours is a pint of bitter,
mine's a Guinness. This proposition is true. We raise
our glasses, we refute it
and refute again.

Shifts Genre Often*

The poet is one who commits
acts of barbarism out of
social urgency. She babbles
and is a rejection of the
language of. She keeps the context
problematic, pivots as often
as possible, which permits
the tide. This is kind of lingo
phrase for those sorts of people lost
in "the water of the river"
when the water *is* the river.
Its maps are metamorphic not
atemporal, a comedy of
metonymic chains, of logics

** For Lyn Hejinian, some of whose presentation in the King's Talks series, King's College London, April 1998, I have paraphrased freely here.*

Become Gems Here

The map has got scrambled & we are all
delighted. My foot is ambiguous, it has
locationality but not
positionality. Don't stop. "Those useful choreographies
can easily become a baleful aerobic"* and
once the stultifiers have a hex on warp agencies
who knows where it'll end up?
But I am certain of a noble uncertainty, it's OK

now I see that you in your way
radiate and this is legal & good.
And everyone says you got the look
of the artist formerly known as god.
We are conversant with our glorious plangent mess
gazing rapidly past this which into here

** The quotation is attributed to Cris Cheek in New Hampshire, September 1996*

Smithereens

This pen has a good sheen to it, or as they say
it's cute as a sack of cash — so in the Rye
Hotel surrounded by smithereens* of popular culture
he set down to write the story of his life.
At my elbow is the most sinister suit I've
seen in a very long while he says these threads is
regal, tell him I'm tied up Mandy I am
shirted & cufflinked up don't get all previous
with me!
            The bar hots up it's actually been
shanghai'd by sweating napes not even a legal
eagle'd wreak a blue streak what can I say?
I meet the brain-dead & the children of the
brain-dead I am among them all the week

** Parts of speech jostling for last orders in Peckham. The shade of the boxer Chris Eubank is lurking in a corner.*

Puissant Car

Like a dickhead in a BMW
he presumes too much—and this presumption
is his puissant car—with copious clocks
and microprocessors, extreme of function.
A male cadence says "just do it" and unkeen
to seem too couth he stupefiedly
obeys and makes the death hex sign to gain
consumer satisfaction, sucked & seen.

My friend! that self-same powerhead within
the chrome & polished steel his glorious armour
was I—gearstick in hand—no, but you can
imagine—liquid years and laddish glamour
faded, carless in Peckham, on your pins
hearing the engine of grace slowly turn over

Speaks into Mobile

Striped of shirt & lambent of tie speaks
into mobile a pipette of value wants to
plug a surf belladonna, becoming
cyclonic, cumuli pile onto his prospect
the heterosexual object of his
desire now once again forbidden
or unrepresentable, smash her face
and centre spread in colour.
COME ON YOU LOVEBIRDS get real
get fucked become the business
take me to your leader, plastic
Schubert in a basket with all the trimmings,
soften my head into the soup of the day
wank to the fascinoma of the month

Click on This

Show me your gold card & I'll show you
my hymen. The modelling of desired behaviours
by a respected role model, irradiated or
genetically modified, can be a key determinant

in changing the whole tone scale
of an individual's attitudes & fragrance.
It is important that this lost language, these
lost sounds are flooded with options.

It is important that these ambient behaviours
are linked to values & competencies, mobile
and integrated into our noise-aspect,

appraisal and fractured management
corporate policies. I have read & understood
and agree to the terms & conditions.

I Go to School in Your Bones*

Sex me up, my shape (she-ape!) of risk
tune up your heels to a serious reciprocity
give me all the attention of your imaginary fingers
like parachute silk in the troposphere.
I refer to your lustrous presence on my arms
where the veins go — apparently distant events —
high scent does enter the frame, with great velocity
I believe it to be nonsense, or else certainty.

Turn up the sound map, a social body
dirtied over from the inheritance
of chaos and loving invention.
Bring me treble clef & metaphor
bind my thresholds and to hell with balance.
Never let I speak —

* *Title taken from Clarissa Pinkola Estés, 'Women Who Run with the Wolves'.*

Windows For Dogs

Thou art my ape, my cynosure,
my star, my dog's bollocks. Mica
winks in the paving stones, my
fingers remember the number

and send graphics, text files & other
information to John. Fibrillating
and seriously flaky. Saw heron fly
onto and perch on a rooftop:

Tulse Hill. More than seven
melodies simultaneously
become chaotic. Two thousand

years pass. An incoming fax. John,
John. The hoarding trembles in the
wind and startles the dog.

Peckham Pulse

In the dusk filled street a man
is up to his wrists in engine.
The Church of Strong Prayer trades
straplines with the Beneficial Veracious
Christ Church. A bad child loudly
bruises the glass. Such journeys
are unbearable from the day they
are born. Something wrong.

Establishing shot across West Africa.

Braids filled with circuits
swing past the shops in holy
brand awareness, bound
to the logic board. Previously unknown
species re-invade.

Broadly Through the Eyes of His Contemporaries

When the film's projected backwards
    mother rises feet-first
from the pool, the twins recede &
    in time all is lost.

White leader, sprocket flicker
    transferred to VHS. Friendship
decays into an exchange of influence
    and services. Chaos follows, then poetry.

Sluice down those monkeys! Put
    the doll back into dark winter,
ramp down the glory. Have key words
    drift from one frame to the next,
but have them marked up as
    unstable & prime for flunking.

Higgledy Piggledy

Back from the deed to the word, no that is
back from the dead to the world
to the brouhaha of bumpy dancers
messed-up tactical dogs & their sunk pints
he crash into the most awful trope in the continuum
on a thin story, not your fault—
Do me a privilege, avoid the brokers
click on here & you're away.
And so how's business? are you sure?
privy to what? the radius of delirium?
Would you say slumped or dumped or
occupationally hazarded? The dancers part company
with their clothes, flatter to deceive, turnover
sluggish—can I do escape?

Without Belief

To keep going on like this how can you live
like this without borders in your head*
as if you were a mollusc or an angel?
The secret's not to try too hard for it's
impossible no chance when everything's
so pitiably sensible & glitters
or fragments in contrast with its label
before attaining maximum velocity

Well I'm not a technical sort of person
in that sense although I'd like to think so—
all I know's sometimes you have this feeling
of architecture, that is, big things heavy
things—and other times there's nothing but
the loudness in your ears or skull of blood

* *Some phrases taken from a magazine interview with the improvising guitarist Caspar Brötzmann.*

The Deep Ecology of Special FX

In the dead weather
before the storm
in fields where copper
flows like butter

as though a small winged
insect were in there
wanting egress
your chest flutters.

In dead television time
a ghost highway links
somewhere to nowhere.

You don't want to be there
but it isn't there—it's here
and there's no place else to go.

Its Ever Moving Shadows

Because I believe in violence lies the answer
and often we have called this love
when I am standing in the light
among the indeterminate connectives
and you come towards me to this blaze that rages
then I touch you on the side of the torso
and on the arm & your face that gazes—
Should I reach your eyes
                                        —but who can say—
I go to sleep in the railway buildings,
patterns of blood flow in the brain
float like surfaces over every ground,
I close my eyes in the transparent universe*
that casts its ever moving shadows—
You have to be lost before you can be found

* *According to Steven Weinberg in* The First Three Minutes, *the universe became transparent to radiation at about 700,000 years of age.*

Big Room

You head for the big room always
tending to lose your marbles at any minute
I can't believe how you—
but shucks, you do have a good eye*
and in & under your wide contemplative sky
if going this way & that you miss
what's closest at hand, ie the thing itself, well then, you can
outstare its palpability
                    By contrast, being a man from the south I'm
                    almost all colour & sound from the inside
                    signifying what? who cares (I do)
                    I come to the power plant & am entranced
                    with the difficulty of it & your actual enigma
                    You bury your head in its clouds

* *The enigma of looking.*

Chaos Theory

South East England contains about 17 people
(and two of these are you & me)
sustainable development, inflated property values.
But we now live in a disinflationary world.

Parts of Arabia had a wet end to last week,
King Khalid military city measured 47mm.
This means downsizing and de-layering
for us, my dear, I'll wager.

You can choose between the headless chickens,
metal with a golden sheen.
It's not that bad, we're talking small percentages.
Over North America, unusual temperatures
made the headlines—
I've a residential cadence yet—

Rug

The business between us is what matters
the recurrent iron & stone the I & the you
and the who and why & whither, a fibre of sense
that oscillates between us we hold onto.
Let's weave that into a metaphor shall we
about six by four, say, a material base
to do the business, the season a little dusty
the night grown old — you want to imagine the rest

Well how's it going and are you ready now

And do you remember how utterly

And was there a time when it might have been

No—there isn't an end to this dialogue, nor will
there be, the stone & iron the iron & stone
again I stand foursquare on the rug you pull

Holding My Heart Still

If I were endlessly
scrutable you could
follow me there
or here—the geography
is immaterial. Then
you could tell me
very gently
what it was

I wanted
/
didn't want
to know:
the story
behind the
story.

I Go to Sleep (3)

Dreaming on tan plush
I view the colour spectrum
the unnecessary repetition
of limiting gestures.
Even now, sentient
screensavers flicker
blindly, false cognates
on the field.

Rooted to the spot
with a mouth full
of language, I am scuppered
by the logic bombs
of double curvature.
O tempora, o fucking mores.

Melancholy

Darling person, whom I had not seen
for many months, I have forgotten so & so's
name, and my words slow down & echo
under the bridge which makes you laugh
it seems as though I am to come to a dead stop.
When things loomed large, we all went mental
with passing & movement, the pageantry
and all that business, when things were future
I mean *in* the future, or of it—
Then quite suddenly it's over, I am a child hearing
Beethoven in the street the evening of Xmas Day
or from summer's vantage watching fall approach, only the years
overlay, and suddenly too there are not many more
to come, my darling person: meetings, partings:

The Book Digs into My Skin

The book digs into my skin & flesh
talks in tongues of petal sound, squeak vapour & dog barks logic
everywhere setting still goes on
when I wasn't quite making sense.
Been down the road & had the man show me
eight machines, feel the strain in my upper body now.
I tried to contact you, but the pulses disappeared
into virtual space, bruising the rationals
all over again, like loops, like dogs, a wind spirals the dust up
"We had magic and
smoke and lots of theater action at that time".*
And then the clocks went back, the lights
went solid rearranged my dental arc into a locked proscenium.
Soon it will be winter you don't reply

* *Taken from* Mixtery, *a festschrift for Anthony Braxton, edited by Graham Lock (Stride, 1995).*

Slaked by Public Water

You are old, father tortoise
spending your end of summer days on a spar
or impersonating one in the
municipal sun of the municipal pond of the
municipal park.*
And there no dog can catch you, prise open your shell
which is a blessing as well as a disguise
when you're practically insensible
and waiting for it to be over.

So that's pretty well it for the season,
planes, sycamores, elders tremble on the brink of shedding
and the goslings almost grown go by on the gloss.
The end of this story is at hand
& is not known

** Peckham Rye Park, perhaps close by where*
the young Blake saw a host of angels in a tree.

They Descry Words, Their Shadows

Goodbye my friends it flows dusks sadly
and reality drops like a stone.
Some members of the group said they admired
someone or something dear to them, it matters
not who was inspired, fit onto standard
postcard size. The liminal space recedes
the question poses limpid as a cry
too late, sat in a garden, one of forks.
                                        So change the script:
The lid falls off the zapper slowly dark
this is where you begin to take apart—
Courage! make stint in the alarm
those impossible journeys struck to brighter lands
at times peaceful and at times without effort

Interrogation Room Remix*

The pillar perished is whereto I leant

A human electricity a great
Generous boom a list

From east to west still seeking though he went

In this grey/yellow space
I sense you
In your best bruiser skin—believe me there's
An alibi in one—

Of all my joy the very bark and rind

In the grey space what I remember's this

The strongest stay of mine unquiet mind
My mind in woe, my body full of smart

And books to read before it grew too late

What can I more but have a woeful heart

* *In memoriam Eric Mottram, 1924–95. With some help from Sir Thomas Wyatt, poem CLX sampled from* Collected Poems, *OUP 1975.*

After Berlioz

Silence … rustle of young wheat
cry of quail
a bunting pouring forth
profound peace … a dead leaf.

Life seemed so very far away
a thing apart
flashed & glinted in the mountings
over there.

And the fit
tearing up handfuls of grass
the crushing sense
of absence
takes possession
as if a vacuum had formed.

Executive Summary

This box of bone & matter
      is
            in the reception area
messaging   speaks into mobile

Friendship decays
                        feels inadequate to
even so
              even this vestige, recombinant

Check:
          press hash 9
then the extension number desired

              fractured,
         her body exploded
as the ground hit it

The Purloined Letter*

Beginning the mountain
with the first basket of earth
is good science.
Exciting counterpoint
from no less than—to some—to many—
is a statement and no statement at all.
Making less most is enriching extent
and there's the special beginning of it.

For your letter and for your view of that Chinese mountain
my own many thanks.
That we are all in
music we are all in poetry we are all
neophytes is encouraging—
and that in its own way completion is begun.

** For Howard Skempton, on his 50th birthday, rearranging or recycling his words in a letter to the author, July 1997.*

Absconscion*

Stay
As though astonished
Through the rubric of
"The transformation of love"†

In the room
In the rain
How you have been
Many times this way O boy

I don't know if I can
Indure
On the door it says

Use other door
You go through it (the
Turn) and

** For Michael Finnissy, on his 50th birthday, July 1996.*
† The phrase is from Rilke's letters.

Astonished in the Flood*

Stay   as though   to sleep
         What sudden   rubric   ripen
I am a   shining   fugitive
         Stay   face and   darken

As though   the known thing   bursts
      Shed energy   rose   froze
Stay tracked   material   personal
      Rare child   depends or   grows

And all our   values hopeful   touch
      That in you   deep   & wanting
To put this   devastated &   to reach

The dark   ally like   slanting
      To each   of us   how much
To sleep   & wake   maybe

* *This title from Michael Haslam's* Continual Song.

Among the Lime Kilns and Dilapidated Pleasure Gardens of Lambeth*

Bebop   Buddleia   backup   crashing   why
        Bring   brouhaha   haha   to the   dark a
Burning   technically   like a   time the lights
        Don't   sleep   sense   shapesh   fish'n

Sense   sensing   lull to   strengths   precise
     Bi biped   peddle   in the   gel if to
You   You don't   And she   I write   unless
     Always   crashing   matter   casts   undo

Darkly wrecked   visible   in parts   perflow
     Delirious   radium   of a   had   & hads
Marine must be   the colours hereto   grows

Delph   germane   unless   a pretty   crowd
       Crashesh   horrid   pellucid   no one   no
Comingundone   crashing   spun to   cloud

* *And this from the pages of Peter Ackroyd's biography,* Blake.

His Last Gasp

You   don't want   but it isn't   there
   As a matter of   muscles   move involuntarily
And   there's nowhere   filled in the   somewhere
   Bright   he can be   flash   momentarily

But lets him   know   why   brightness moves
   How he can be   but isn't   fetch the air
Which   isn't here   how   devastate behoves
   Of all significant   places   personally   rare

Oh known thing   Oh air   that multiplies   the known
   Oh technical adventure   given hinterland   bestir
Go into vehicle   given   grown

To thrive &   spasm   else to be   gone
   Want is   distance   dust hereto   there
Simply suck   illuminate   eliminate   alone

His Last Gasp (2)

but isn't
matter
nowhere
Bright

know
the air
Which isn't
person

know Oh air
adventure given

To
Want is to
illuminate

A Friend in Need

The windows smashed
and the vase
                                        that you, a woman thus
Poor Tom—

I love my love with a el
"or maybe shut your face"*
It just isn't fair
                                        or graceful

that you should—
oh   my dear
friend in the   world

Oh maybe kiss
before I go to ground in the vertical
desert   like this

* *JHP, of course.*

Four*

One is to become
The other—it never happened
A third—relatively minor
And after all, the last
It did not change my life
From east to west still seeking though he went
Suppose that it, or they, can, will & did or do
Then all would be—otherwise
          If not now when
          If not when, then
          Why
          If not, well then
          How
          But why not now?

* *After listening to* The Crowd, *Rova saxophone quartet, Hat Hut CD. For a far more comprehensive response to the same, see Clark Coolidge's* The Rova Improvisations *(Sun & Moon, 1994).*

Eventually Get Up and Go

Thinking
lay across one of the thwarts
how long
the
water

And that it was
they should come
by such a little to my body

I live free
and can escape thither when this
the empty downland then
under the wind
is a mood that comes to
myself from the confusion*

* *From the final pages of H G Wells'* The Island of Dr Moreau

PART II

Serious Jungle

Already bicameral, unflummoxed amid breccia
or is it bric-à-brac, you return to your passions
a quizzical bunny, bouncing to the strange
attractors of the city, parrotty and fruity to boot
Chromatic with butterflies re-engined for timing
fashioned to be daffy of absolute value, akimbo
with the loveliness of an open door
lashings of snippets dance to your jungle beat
And when you run to the end of the jungle
let not your value be exchanged
let your kilter remain in the limbo of joy
till dusk has reclaimed the farthest shore
Abre las puertas por favor
*quiero olvidar lo que es dolor**

* *The last two lines are from a popular song from Ecuador.*

Black Dog

He steps through the door. The emblems
are on his forehead, the molecules of sadness
in his mouth. I heard laughing & thunder
in the night before he arrived.

How sharply I feel the bite, how quickly
how trembling I make my way over to you
across the long prairie bed, in the
long rumbling dawn that never ends…

In the republic of dreams in the dry bed
in terror as the colours change always
where trash is thrown you menstruate

out of the night the breakers the laughter
the beach at the end of the road that never ends.
I'll wait for you there don't let me down.

Three

Three is two & one
The octave—never harboured
Or heard—reflectively finer
And before all, the past
"You must change your life"
The pillar perished is whereto I leant
Suppose I had not, turned I did into undo
Then all would be—restored
    If not the one
    Or two, when
    You
    Were not, well then
    Who
    Am I now?

Too Chicken to Talk Turkey

I love speech, and most of all
the shape it makes in your mouth.
Or: I love speech, and in particular
the way that your mouth shapes it.

It's your mouth, and mine
and the shapes that emerge
then make a text, or a reply. I wish I could say.
And I am so sorry.
And I rejoice. On the slow curtain, dusk
begins to gather, in the park men walk
their dogs
and the scent of hot wax fades in the room.
Such happiness awaits us.
(This happiness will end.)

Red Shoes

Red shoes black shoes every kind
of shoes *Dance on my friend!* as we elapse
from coma to wakefulness along the river
side we are really just talking and walking and
talking nothing more and nothing more
is needed bursting heart to heart to
think of it! that you should be a friend in the
world is everything (blue shoes a lapsed kiss)—
Who can say
it drifts and skips is fortunate and is
three words your peaceful embouchure
for many years the vertical desert
of the treble clef I think it has been happening
for many years

Your Peaceful Embouchure

In respect of a place I loved and was in that
I now return to or open to, it's wonderful
how you in your body
and I in you, how normal it is.
And this becomes a morning you inhabit
always these days as the sun ascends—
it was as though it always has, and is
the love of evermore being guided.
Since it has come to beam on us I find it
in me to cope, packed into small pitches as I am
staggering into & out of my clothes
burning to tell as never before
living to be in the solid deep
swaddled and watching, so early days.

In the Light of

I am   in England but
not of it   you could be
    a travelling player
echo-accoutred   your eyes
glistening with gaze aforethought
in the dark   my head listening
to its own beat or become then aware
of yours the metal device against your good heart.

And there were also
    lambent key sequences, or sequins
against the squeaking floorboard.
Who can recall the light
    of dwelling   in memory before
the thing had happened, even?

Blue Day

Brave and excellent as you are, you'll know
what's broached must also be consumed profusely.
All that robust energy, and the narrative on an
arbitrary grid.
                    A greybeard named Zeno
                         asks what happened? I don't
recall, he said, I will do some creative work today
but it was too complete and had too much meaning
                    to be useful.
                                   Us lugging our rucks
them selling late repros at high prices,
stock collapsed, Niagara in our bellies.
      Soon healed.
Draw the curtains on a blue day today, wield
blue dangerously before it stretches

I'm Doing My Books on You

Oh pedal point, oh search engine
show me your autumnal grief caboodle
your body at the velocity of zero
your loved voice superimposed.
Oh mobile antenna, heavenly brico-
lage my things, my autumnal things.
No. They are not
mine, they never were, & suddenly there you are:
what mambos what ecliptics
so out of & in control. (The body of course
is one's writing, or properly,
what writes this: it comes from somewhere.)
          Oh pedal point
          Oh embouchure

Out in the Violets

Allure is being cancelled each day as I speak
and I can't hardly talk
            How do us talk
about I & you?

            This box doesn't deserve to think!

They are partly rehydrated
figs ready to eat now

                        Out at sea
a rockpool the Dardanelles as a child
peers out on beauty

bells chime & float towards too much

out in the violets & the mud
listening to cuckoos

The Birth Ship

The lovers are entwined one on the other
breathing together they produce
the same note.
Someone cries

out in the night.   There is nothing
outside themselves
This does not
appal them as it should.

They produce offspring
who grow up eventually and pursue
independent careers.

Someone dies   The window can't
easily be opened.   Outside
themselves the world moves

Mercy

Throw yourself on my mercy, and I'll throw myself
    upon yours. Then we'll enter into
the summer of it with all due sumptuousness
    and imperturbability. But you
already know this. Here begins the realm
    of the first person plural: impossibility
coming into its pomp, the one & the other making
    a collective pronoun of the "enemy self"*—

we cannot know just what that person's thinking.
    Here begins the realm of imposs-
ibility, you know it, not that, not that
    but this, that we're immersed in, where
we learn it from, the actual stuff
    not rockets & bells, not that, but this,
                                        this...

* *Laura Riding, "As Many Questions As Answers".*

A Dream of Reclaimed Land

Time knows it   equivalence knows it
the filth know it   mine host behind the bar
knows it   the helix of language knows it
surplus value knows it   the boys who
take care of these things know it
Mary Quite Contrary, the twin strikers, the midnighters
all know it   Trace who is 4 Gary knows it
numbers melody mayhem & transformation know it

But you my beauty who find yourself in a place
vastly crammed with incident and resource, and see
no way out of it, you do not know it.
You venture onto "reclaimed land" but it's dark to you:

ahead, huge buildings with screens on which luminous text
scrolls & forever transforms, yet seems hardly to change.

You Move Your Hands

Oh my
        dearest person what it is you mean
to me and all
        that I entail—

To awaken in the early
        hours of the day near the
loved one
        it is too much to bear.

Crotales. Untuned percussion. From afar:
        ostinati, the return of thunder.
Then a low, held note.

You move your hands
        in the air   like this—
You shine from the face outward.

A Wedding*

flowered out of nowhere
and overwhelmed
the groundwork—
it's just that events conspired.
A thin sliver of pale blue on the western
horizon & a white cotton shirt
over the heart.
And so it proved

The path of totality
brought us here†
to the churchyard. The bloom
of voices came
through. Once & for all
it was

* *The following sequence uses material from Stravinsky's 'Les Noces'.*
† *Solar eclipse partly visible in London, 11 August 1999.*

A Wedding (2)

On Wednesday the corona
On Thursday a strange & hilarious day
On Friday my green gardens are blooming
On Saturday the sky was fresh

O braid my
light-brown braid
I plaited you mechanically
with the words of consolation.
One braid
becomes two,
the army
of mechanicals
arrive—
attacca subita

A Wedding (3)

And so it proved: they approached
in such a space, believing that
this time was never to have arrived.
But, having come, it stays just long enough

to make a resonance in the air.
          Speech forms,
a trumpet line ascends into
imaginary sunlight at the clerestory.

The tablecloth
The corona the
return of war—

Abstraction: the imaginary
          combination
of line & light

A Wedding (4)

Someone is choosing his words
          Sudden rain, and thunder
We're loose in a room
          Someone plucks up courage
to be composed, to be where
nobody expected. Another fumbles
and a third says
          "Take your time"

A hand, a flower, a sweet,
a fruit, a violet, short-lived,
unannounced.

Someone moves across
the garden, as she'd done when a girl.
That was in the photograph.

A Wedding (5)

We are talking as
night returns, "I
don't know whether
I can get to
sleep." We shall have to
get into our clothes,
go out, post letters,
return as though

Sparrow to sparrow
lay a sound
upon a sound.
We live by day
& night, we practise
hospitality.

A Wedding (6)

but here there is only a
light breeze ruffles the
            water out of
            darkness—

The future returns
with enhanced
            energy
as a consequence of it,
            money
dwindling, weather changeable.
Someone takes a picture,
someone
            is full of business, gradually
the clouds dispersed

Two

Now am I whom artifice
Supposes? Were you then, two
Or one if not restored? well then
Would all undo into I did,
Pitch into bliss, had I not turned?
The pillar perished is whereto I leant
Your change must be before all, relatively heard
Or harboured, octave one & two
          If not this, then
          This
          A pair, as one—
          Or not, the one
          And two
          Is one

One to One: Nourishment

On a blue day, one has food and passes it to
the other. It's a spoon, and there is food on it.
Dirt is postponed. Each is halfway between.
The food is made of molecules—proteins & fats—
it enters and is appropriate to the function, it
does not overstay. The gesture is one of
appeasement, of intimacy and proffered friendship.
Tombstones come down, milk forms, it's only

human. One begins and the other completes
the task begun. Receiving is likewise,
reciprocal sluices: the other responds generously
to the one, and this is what was intended. You are
valued, for your lips curl round my gift.
What is freely offered

One to Many: Interpretation

We are constituted, and so we are free.
Who says? The person whose voice
so distorts that no information is conveyed?
And the others, assembled on this platform
or that one, contemplating icons, of a morning?
It's windy. Delays are occurring. Globalisation
occurs. In Antarctica, an iceberg the size of
Wales starts to break up.

The broadcast server will close down
in 1 minute—please save your data.
This is security. The fire alarm tests
have now been completed and
normal procedures are back in operation.
You have new mail waiting.

Many to One: Sound Production

Extremely rapid & akin. Dental tremoli:
the lower jaw trembles to create amplitude.
There is extensive use of glissandi. I love
the way in which the air is set in motion
in the movements of the organs in which
it vibrates between. It is as if coupled,
turns on the role, the middle & final
metamorphic hinges where the text shape changes.
Her virtuosity deployed, each sound is followed
by a very long pause, whose extremes are
as at the extremes.
                                        It is as if uncommon
ground whose extremes have no text. That
she might compose and that this might lead to

Many to Many: Big Story

Those of us remaining on the bus no longer have recourse to the big story. Already, as it begins to traverse the bridge, the passengers fall into a sweve wherein their several *Is* become ball-bearings floating freely in the roof, a concatenation of little stories (neither the dialectic of the Spirit, nor even the emancipation of humanity), separated only by the Walkman's pause button. Already the *Is* are becoming *Yous*, reaching further and further, till too soon it's too much. And so on and on, etc *ad infinitum* whatever happened to *dichten* = *condensare* for fuck's sake?

At Aldgate, Zeno leaves his seat and descends the stairwell, sumptuously apparelled. Thames glitter on a moving horizon, light brown and done in. His story over, he has succeeded in showing that the bus will never reach the opposite bank.

Rapturous Hazard

A man breathes, and breathes again. A person who is anxious to arrive but getting there slowly. Oh, so *that's* what's going on. He doesn't care what the time is nor what the idea might be. Some might have attempted diagnosis, but not he. Once might have been, got control, working through, can think about, did have the same but not madly keen. It's been a brilliant thing, yet transient and you can make something of it. It was his very much last moment.

As for her, she could need something to feel, or to deal with. That could be the problem. The marks she made in the air have faded. The thought she made in the mouth comes into being. She turns to it again. "The importance of material process over representation."

Hazardous Rapture

He needs out, or sorted. Done no work. It was a relationship, actually charged and personal. Something actually changed. He partially goes to work, it's a book that minds him. Fired, or what? He watches them leave the room, to work or talk, allowing paper to rustle behind, or glass to rest on wood. Not enough time, that's for sure.

She's taken a deep angle to a short problem, but would like to get seriously. That could be a possibility. The catering is indifferent, but friendship flowers. She turns to it for the first time. He's jumped a barrier. Why should anyone believe her?

Ruptured Horizon

Walks by a stream, rebuffed and unaware of the impending. Indifferent weather might intervene. So what? Questions of scale, built on distance. Waterboatmen skip endlessly nested paragraphs. "Occlusion of the middle ground, the ground of bourgeois realism, allows the large-scale to merge with the small." A man lays his clarinet on the floor, shuffles inclement pages prior to uttering. It was very much improvised.

A woman taps on the sculpture and listens to the sound it makes. The hills slope away. Woodland enfolds a helix of rapid transformations. Mingling with others in the canteen while songsters brood on the outside. That could be the answer. A patina of rust accumulates over a period of years, allowing hermeneutic possibilities and preventing the formation of narrative.

In Lithuania*

Can hear, can feel and see
and do human voices,
perform all manner of ventriloquial tricks
as though the leaves were not falling
and importunate singers
were not echoing round
with bass voices licking the vast spaces
of the ears
and rocks were not silent
nor light reflecting
on church bells tolling in the morning.

The bell is the only instrument
that does not possess the complete harmonic series.
Which is why it sounds sad.†

* *Poetry Autumn in Druskininkai, October 2000.*
† *I am indebted to Gregory Rose for this observation.*

In Lithuania (2): To the Addressee

Thickly yellow, leaves continue to fall
upon my head. Some people link birches with banners.
Loud accordion music, *ad lib*.
A fisherman, then a mother & child
move off the riverbank to make way.

Some people, at the pink hotel.
The white riverboat. On a bench
BIELAS IS COOL. A tower
in the blue sky, extraordinary concrete.

How I wish you were here to share
this blue day that emerges. Hush.

A rustling
as of leaves that rush forever through trees.
                                                                        Then pause.
I shall meet you at the approaching time.

Glints in a Path

Poetic
artifice
comme il faut
the bridge
of size
(which matters not)

We have perfect
bliss to
pitch in
this
our perfect
life
as one, a pair —
too brief!

The Nostalgia for Presence Felt by the Human Subject

They've all gone
    the big stories.
Let's not mourn
    them
        we can live
and be
    without
them and within our lives

as in those outsize
        storms
in which the clouds
        and we cling
only to that—
    to us through

Pleated Glory

Pleated in
love & awe
                    I can't
                                escape I
                    "know" it
but the
            mind this body's
            attached to

wanders
            to the last
day of
breathing
                    which is
                    the frame

Perturbations

You (a person)
at the keyboard (or away
from it). As if poised for flight
            to lee of, great hush.
The wood in that floor
with a solid sheen to it
your feet, pointed
inward

Circumambient

sour
green cymbals are stroked
with great, great gentleness (*ppp*)
to produce longing (*keening*).

This ruins my eyes.

Perturbations (2)

…linger, petal
        we have a great
deal to do.

The sound of rain,
        or a rainstick.
A sizzle through
        the serial port.

All over the planet, a low
        drumming on wood
and some stuff
        on the E string, high…

…linger,
        petal.
Don't furl.

Perturbations (3)

Enter the poet, stage left.

I see her anew
as you pass through the door

you are so like…

          His things his beautiful things
          His books his cathedral

          something that was, & no longer is.
          All fall down.

There is no
thing that may be compared. (Nothing
is comparable.)
                    The trombones bark:
Vanity!
          Vanity!
                    Vanity!

Perturbations (4)

"The night is blue"   and the season
a little dusty   but we begin as always
with not heeding and coming in just on the hour
in ones & twos to gather and approach
the question of intent
                              / and all those others—
For if there were no questions to cluster round
why then our skins would sink into the prevailing
gold, scribbling to oblivion.

What extraordinary advent-
ure it all is. A blue PowerBook,
an electronic skin to skim upon.

                                        The moonlight, etc.
                                        Sounds of birds & monkeys.
                                        Sounds of the Far East.

Perturbations (5)

Perhaps sounds briefly made, or gestures
and then with the flat of the hands
so thoroughly as to come to some sort of
recognition, caressing
with backs of the hands and backs of the fingers
with the side of the fists. And was struck

by how dance-like the movement
in passion frenzy giving shape to
or suffering injury
with elbows and leaning
did not seem to refer, just hit & hit again.

And briefly standing quietly, and then again
with chopping motion, not in unison.

I would never hurt you.

Perturbations (6)

It begins here, the end of it—
You will call out
in your unknowing
at the climacteric or vertex

You were supposed to be there, and you were
for a structure'd collapsed
and everything in all directions
started uttering and had nearly blown away

You will call out, perhaps sounds
          briefly made too, with
          wooden implements who
can say, who knows
          the many kinds and ways
          the trade winds—

Perturbations (7)

Those great rich blacks come back
                                        in noirish imper-
                    turbable notations of the body.
The pale blue upright I appears at centre
of the screen,* there being that warmth

and difficulty. I think she grew to be broken
her eyes wide open do you remember that
lustrous silence

Immense patterns of 1s and 0s appear

there is that sound of wind
and even further away are muffled drums & a wist-
                    ful woodwind theme
as if loveliness might be stepped on, or
limbs as seen close up, and slightly out
of focus. But two hundred years have passed!
                    We cut to an empty†

* *The opening credits.*
† *Here the film breaks.*

Da Capo, Which Means, Out of My Head

On the box we find
celestial messages from splendid empires

There's been a death in the family
And then there was one

so madly set a thesis burned the toast
SLAM on the brakes
whoo—
(a paradox)

(A non-expanding universe would
actually entail even worse paradoxes)
Like like like—
This is where we learn impossibility from
This box this box this box this
One to one to one

One

Now, not why
But how—then well, not if
Why then, when not
If when, now not
If otherwise—be?
Would all then do or did & will?
Can they or it that suppose
went he though seeking still?
west to east from
life my change nor
did it last, all after
and minor, relatively third—
it happened never, other to
become is one

Six Songs
of the Children of Abraham

2008

i.m. Bill Griffiths

1

we sham & pretend sickness
hedge-robbers & strippers of children
or perhaps we poor
going naked or at least hardly
no clothes on our back
bare armed & bare legged
our hair is long & filthily knotted
a staff in our cheating hands
yet we will say
how piteously and most extremely
we have been beaten

2

outside the Crown
Bank Holiday Monday
a lusty strong rogue they say
queer cove & all
who feigneth himself mad and carrieth a pack of wool
or a stick or such like toy
I see the straw hanging upon thy cap & coat
face stares like a Saracen
smoking a fag no care for a ban
conversing to women & children
out the corner of's mouth
and a withered greyhound in a shirt
laid on the pavement with them others
in the name of Rawhead or Bloodybones
some of these be merry & very pleasant
some others be as cold & reasonable
to talk with all
as a banker with's PIN & plastic
and empty toxic promises

3

hungry ghosts
antickly tricked-up with ribbons, red tape, foxtails, rags
we amuse you
fling dust in your eyes
from our pockets
or from imagination strange tales
of drowning & running over
then our comrade under the notion of pity
would lay his hand on whatever came near
rooky rooking you angels
delicate as you like

4

bluffers & divers, dukes & gills
down on our luck
says we done this that or t'other
for which banged up
yet not one in twenty was in prison for any such cause
a sheet about's bodys
hanging to the hams, bandolier-wise
them walking up & down the country more terribly
we will dance & sing & sing
and dance till the thing
runs out
so that in the finish when us come
up before the beak
queer cuffin, hoggish & choleric
there'll be the end to this dance
be hanging be the neck

5

you will not be rid of us
we will pick or steal poultry or linen
will demand bacon, cheese or wool
or anything that is worth money
with the fierce countenance of a football supporter
down the Shed or North Bank as't'was
in days of youth
mojos & pins stuck into our flesh
to excite pity
and all women that wander be at our commandment
wee veteran vagrants, tramps
in the wind & the rain
bound for England's glory for
salivation in a digital shadow in a
tidal basin of TV celebrity
you will not be rid of us for we are
heading for Abraham's balsam

6

give me my slate & put it round
me carcase of no account
the flesh of arms or back
shall be scarce covered as I booze
my last
I say it is small & naughty drink
light of the morning to you

Afterword

A *Collected Poems* is a tombstone – there's no getting away from that. So it was with decidedly mixed feelings that I approached this project. But it has to be said this is a good moment to pause and take stock; it's been a while now since verse composition was central to my practice, and the work of some forty years can be looked back on with some degree of objectivity, now that I am no longer fabricating lines, but rather sentences (though there are a lot of those here too). (Works consisting entirely or mainly of sentences, such as *Bardo* (Knives, Forks & Spoons Press, 2011) and *a book with no name* (Shearsman Books, 2016) are excluded.)

The continuity with the previous collection, *No Public Language: Selected Poems 1975–1995*, is evident. Once again, the poems are presented in the form of their original, separately published books, and all those included there are present here, with the addition of others to fill out the history. I tend to compose in books, as I said then. And most of those books are now either out of print, or in a few cases were never actually published as I had intended. I hope they have a decent after-life in these pages.

Resources

Erik Satie loved children – A tiny pamphlet from my own Share Publications, from a period documented in *Wild Metrics* (Grand Iota, 2019).

Dover – Likewise.

Lorca: an elegiac fragment – First published under the Alembic Editions imprint (with Robert Hampson and Peter Barry). Notes on the sequence are included, as in the original, within the body of the text.

Tilth – Several texts and films fertilised this project, principally among them 'Kubla Khan' – which is also used as the main structural device.

Drumming & Poems – 'Old Man, Camberwell' uses material from an unpublished set of interviews with people who live alone; the last six lines of 'Poster, Walworth Rd' are taken verbatim from an interview with the TV playwright Dennis Potter; 'What the razor knew' slices material from J W Dunne, Val Wilmer, Jacques Monod; 'Southall' is from eye-witness accounts, mainly by Asians, of the riots of April 1979; 'Drumming (Slow Return)' was written during the passage through Parliament of the Nationality Bill in winter 1980/81, and refers to the three classes of citizenship proposed by the Bill; section 2 of the poem is based on reminiscences by Isaac Gordon, a Jamaican immigrant; the poem is an elegy to Blair Peach, a teacher beaten to death by police on 23 April 1979 during an anti-fascist demonstration.

Intensive Care – The Takahashi poem quoted at the head of 'Intensive Care' is 'Canna' from *Afterimages* (1972); 'Total Allergy Syndrome' quotes Elvis Costello in stanza 2, and the Boulez quote is from a TV documentary; 'Listen to Britain' takes its title from the Humphrey Jennings wartime documentary; 'Shadow of White Days' refers to Bach's unfinished *Art of Fugue*; 'Five Nocturnes' was written after an exhibition of Derek Jarman's paintings at the ICA, London, 1984; 'The Great Tradition' quotes Jacques Lacan via Fredric Jameson's *The Prison House of Language*, also *Class Struggles in South London 1850–1900* (Southwark-Lambeth History Workshop, 1980), *The Spirit of London's River* by L M Bates (1980) and *Anchor and Hope* by Jo Anderson (1981); Lord Devonport was chairman of the Port of London Authority and the Spike was Camberwell Workhouse, later Camberwell DHSS Resettlement Centre, closed in 1985.

A4 Portrait and **A4 Landscape** – Conceived as the thesis and antithesis to be resolved in *3600 Weekends'* synthesis. It didn't quite work out that way. The original premise of *A4 Portrait* was that the writing should be generated spontaneously on a daily basis, with erasure being the only permitted editorial function.

Lyrical Ballets – Originally a pamphlet from Torque Press (1990), later collected in *Songbook* (Shearsman Books, 2009).

Good Science – Subtitled *Poems 1983–1991* and published by Roof Books, New York. Written in South London, Cambridge, Suffolk, Luxembourg and southern Spain during that period. Notes to 'Lexical Dub' (of which there was once an audio version released as a cassette by Balsam Flex) are included in the body of the text; other notes on resources are now lost.

3600 Weekends – The epigraph to 'Experimentally' is a description of the working methods of the film-maker Rainer Werner Fassbinder; the Swedish prime minister in 'Fugitively' was Olof Palme; 'In the Japanese Fashion' pastiches Basho; a zoetrope ('Spirit Voices') is a child's toy and also the wheel of life.

Glissando Curve – This book was to have been published in the late 1990s by Sun & Moon in the USA, but the press went into liquidation before that could happen. Most of the poems were first collected in 2006 within the pages of *No Public Language*; three were originally published separately as *Bird Migration in the 21st Century* by Spectacular Diseases in the same year. 'Ghazal of the Gun' samples text from an article by Dr Harold Hillman, reprinted in *The Independent on Sunday*, April 1995 – the poem is dedicated to Dylan Coffey; 'Arabesque

Harmonics': a famous *cante jondo* singer claimed that when her muse was really cooking her mouth felt as though it were full of blood; 'Interference Ghazal' is aborted at line 6; 'Alborada of Late Capitalism': an *alborada* is a dawn song (=*aubade*); 'Approaching the House of Béla Bartók' was written following a visit in 1991 to the house Bartók lived in from 1931–42, at 29 Csalán Road, Budapest, now preserved as a museum – the poem uses Bartók's favoured arch structure, 3(c) representing the apex of the curve, where it turns back from silence; 'Immigrant Music' draws on the film *Latcho Drom* (Safe Journey), about the Gypsy diaspora; 'Wave Ghazal' from newspaper reports from the Balkans, 1993; 'An Imaginary Landscape' from Paul Klee via Harrison Birtwistle, written while listening to the latter's awesome *Earth Dances*, shortly after the first Gulf War; 'Sizewell Ghazal' was written in Suffolk, during construction of Sizewell "B" nuclear power station; 'Brilliant Sojourn' is another poem from Suffolk, generated by a seed vocabulary from Pierre Boulez, *Orientations*, 1986; the diva was Elisabeth Söderström, the "exiled Russians" the Borodin Quartet, in residence at Snape; notes to 'Bird Migration in the 21st Century' are included within the text.

Chaconne – Written in the mid-1990s and published online as an e-book by Shearsman Books in 2007 and later collected in *Songbook*. It is inspired by Bach's 'Chaconne' from the 2nd Partita for unaccompanied violin and by mediaeval Spanish music. In the poem, a sequence of 49 syllabic line-patterns cycles through a five-line stanza form, making a total of 49 stanzas without repetition. Titles of many compositions by John Coltrane are interwoven.

Red: Narrative Poem – Collected in *Songbook*, together with a printed score of my own musical setting, it was written in 1998–9, and performed by Elaine Randle (later Elaine Edwards) and me, together with versions of three poems from *eight + six* (see below) with music by Elaine, in the SubVoicive poetry reading series in London in March 1999, and at the Huddersfield Poetry Festival in October that year. 'Red' was also published in *a-a-a-a-a*, a journal of the Contemporary Poetry Workshop at Birkbeck College, London, with an accompanying CD containing a performance by Elaine and myself.

Songs of the Permanent Way – These date from around 2000 and were first published in *Songbook*.

The Glory Boxes – Another book that never appeared. The sequence is printed in its entirety for the first time here. The *Glory Boxes* are devices or instruments from which diverse melodies may be derived. Though discrete entities, their self-replenishing content also flows between each Box: thus, the last line of each flows back into its first, but also into the first line of the next. The last line of the last Box flows into the first of the first. The first Box uses two voices in a kind of counterpoint, then follow two Boxes with three voices and three Boxes with four voices. The voices are distinguished visually by their alignment on the page, and the piece may be (and has been) performed by four speakers. The sources of the texts are as follows: Fred Adams, *The Five Ages of the Universe* (1999); Pierre Boulez, *Boulez on Music Today* (1975); John Cage, 'Metamorphosis' (1938); Jack Cohen & Ian Stewart, *The Collapse of Chaos* (1994); Peter Coveney & Roger Highfield, *The Arrow of Time* (1990); Antonio R Damasio, 'How the Brain Creates the Mind' in *Scientific American*, December 1999; James Gleick, *Chaos* (1988); David Goode, *Wild in London* (1986); W. H. Hudson, *Birds in London* (1928); Lucretius, *On the Nature of Things* Book 3 (1st century BC, tr. Martin Ferguson Smith, 1969); M. Merleau-Ponty, *Phenomenology of Perception*, tr. Colin Smith (1962); Roger Penrose, *The Emperor's New Mind* (1989); Tom Raworth, *Eternal Sections* (1993); R. M. Rilke, from letter to Witold von Hulewicz, 13 November 1925; James E. Whinnery, 'Induction of Conciousness in the Ischemic Brain' and David J Chalmers, 'Facing Up to the Problem of Consciousness' in Hameroff et al (ed.) *Toward a Science of Consciousness* (1996); William Wordsworth, 'Ode: Intimations of Immortality' (1807); Theodore Zeldin, *An Intimate History of Humanity* (1995).

There's Something in There – Written to a commission by the pianist John Tilbury, and forming the basis of his work for voice, piano and electronics which was premiered at Leeds Town Hall in July 2003. A CD was planned, but never appeared, though Colin Still (Optic Nerve) privately distributed a few copies. Collected in *Songbook.*

eight + six – Published in 2003 by Reality Street Editions. Notes integral to the text. The poems reference the sonnet form (as the title indicates) and the sequence also follows the eight : six ratio, with the 98 poems divided into sections of 56 and 42.

Six Songs of the Children of Abraham – Written in response to a call from David Annwn for *The Canting Academy* (2008), an anthology of writing inspired by Richard Head's 17th century dictionary of criminal slang. Later collected in *Songbook.*

www.ingramcontent.com/pod-product-compliance
Lightning Source LLC
Chambersburg PA
CBHW030040240426
43667CB00035B/84
9781848617605